Tide and Current Glossary

U.S. DEPARTMENT OF COMMERCE
Norman Mineta, Secretary

National Oceanic and Atmospheric Administration
D. James Baker, Administrator

National Ocean Service
Margaret Davidson, Assistant Administrator

Center for Operational Oceanographic Products and Services
David M. Kennedy, Acting Director

Preface to 1999 Edition

The publication is a revision of the 1989 edition. This edition has been a group effort by Steacy D. Hicks, Richard L. Sillcox, C. Reid Nichols, Brenda Via, and Evette C. McCray. It was subsequently revised by Chris Zervas. Final formatting, layout, and printing has been under the authority of Brenda Via.

The author wishes to thank the following for their contributions: C. Reid Nichols (numerous entries), Richard L. Sillcox, Jack E. Fancher, Dr. Robert G. Williams, Thomas J. Kendrick, Douglas M. Martin, David B. Zilkoski, Richard Edwing, Michael Szabados, Steven Lyles, James Hubbard, Michael Gibson, Steven Gill, William Stoney, Dr. Ledolph Baer, and Dr. Bruce B. Parker. Special thanks is given to Dr. Kurt Hess for his numerous technical corrections and suggestions.

Printing History of Tide and Current Glossary

Special Publication No. 228, Coast and Geodetic Survey, by Paul Schureman, 1941.

Special Publication No. 228, Coast and Geodetic Survey, by Paul Schureman revised by E. C. McKay and F. J. Haight, 1949.

Special Publication No. 228, Coast and Geodetic Survey, by Paul Schureman, reprinted with corrections, 1963.

National Ocean Survey, by Paul Schureman, revised by Steacy D. Hicks, 1975.

National Ocean Service, by Steacy D. Hicks, 1984.

National Ocean Service, by Steacy D. Hicks, 1989.

National Ocean Service, by Steacy D. Hicks, 1999.

For further information on tides, sea level, tidal datums, record certifications, and related publications, contact:

NOAA, National Ocean Service
CO-OPS, Products and Services N/OPS3
Attn: User Services
1305 East-West Highway
Silver Spring, MD 20190-3281

Phone: (301)713-2877 Ext. 176
Fax: (301)713-4437

For further information on Great Lakes water levels, datums, and related publications, contact:

NOAA, National Ocean Service
CO-OPS, Requirements and Development N/OPS1
Attn: Great Lakes
1305 East-West Highway
Silver Spring, MD 20910-3281

Phone: (301)713-2902 Ext. 184
Fax: (301)713-4435

For further information on currents, tide and tidal current predictions, and related publications, contact:

NOAA, National Ocean Service
CO-OPS, Products and Services N/OPS3
Attn: Tidal Predictions
1305 East-West Highway
Silver Spring, MD 20910-3281

Phone: (301)713-2815 Ext. 119
Fax: (301)713-4500

Tide and Current Glossary

A

absolute mean sea level change—An eustatic change in mean sea level relative to a conventional terrestrial coordinate system with the origin at the center of mass of the Earth.

accepted values—Tidal datums and Greenwich high and low water intervals obtained through primary determination or comparison of simultaneous observations with a control tide station in order to derive the equivalent value that would be obtained with a 19-year series.

acoustic Doppler current profiler (ADCP)—A current measuring instrument employing the transmission of high frequency acoustic signals in the water. The current is determined by a Doppler shift in the backscatter echo from plankton, suspended sediment, and bubbles, all assumed to be moving with the mean speed of the water. Time gating circuitry is employed which uses differences in acoustic travel time to divide the water column into range intervals, called bins. The bin determinations allow development of a profile of current speed and direction over most of the water column. The ADCP can be deployed from a moving vessel, tow, buoy, or bottom platform. In the latter configuration, it is nonobtrusive in the water column and thus can be deployed in shipping channels.

ADR gauge—Analog to Digital Recording water level gauge. A float or pressure-actuated water level gauge that records heights at regular time intervals in digital format.

age of diurnal inequality—The time interval between the maximum semimonthly north or south declination of the Moon and the maximum effect of declination upon range of tide or speed of the tidal current. The age may be computed from the harmonic constants by the formula:
age of diurnal inequality = $0.911(K_1^\circ - O_1^\circ)$ hours.

age of Moon—The time elapsed since the preceding new Moon

age of parallax inequality—The time interval between perigee of the Moon and the maximum effect of parallax upon range of tide or speed of the tidal current. This age may be computed from the harmonic constants by the formula:
age of parallax inequality = $1.837(M_2^\circ - N_2^\circ)$ hours.

age of phase inequality—The time interval between new or full Moon and the maximum effect of these phases upon range of tide or speed of the tidal current. This age may be computed from the harmonic constants by the formula:
age of phase inequality = $0.984(S_2^\circ - M_2^\circ)$ hours.

age of tide—Same as age of phase inequality.

agger—Same as double tide.

Agulhas Current—An Indian Ocean current setting southwestward along the southeast coast of Africa.

air acoustic ranging sensor—A pulsed, acoustic ranging device using the air column in a tube as the acoustic sound path. The fundamental measurement is the time it takes for the acoustic signal to travel from a transmitter to the water surface and then back to the receiver. The distance from a reference point to the water surface is derived from the travel time. A calibration point is set at a fixed distance from the acoustic transducer and is used to correct the measured distance using the calibrated sound velocity in the tube. Air temperature sensors are located in the protective well for the purpose of verifying uniformity of temperature for measurements taken by the air acoustic ranging sensor.

Alaska Current—A North Pacific Ocean current setting counterclockwise along the coasts of Canada and Alaska in the Gulf of Alaska.

Alaskan Stream—A North Pacific Ocean current setting westward along the south side of the Aleutian Islands. It is an extension of the Alaska Current.

amphidromic point—A point of zero amplitude of the observed or a constituent tide.

amphidromic region—An area surrounding an amphidromic point from which the radiating cotidal lines progress through all hours of the tidal cycle.

amplitude (H)—One-half the range of a constituent tide. By analogy, it may be applied also to the maximum speed of a constituent current.

analog—A continuous measurement or a continuous graphic display of data. See ADR gauge and marigram.

analysis, harmonic—See harmonic analysis.

analyzer, harmonic—See harmonic analyzer.

angular velocity of the Earth's rotation (Ω)—Time rate of change of angular displacement relative to the fixed stars. It is equal to $0.729,211 \times 10^{-4}$ radian/second.

annual inequality—Seasonal variation in water level or current, more or less periodic, due chiefly to meteorological causes.

anomalistic—Pertaining to the periodic return of the Moon to its perigee or the Earth to its perihelion. The anomalistic month is the average period of the revolution of the Moon around the Earth with respect to lunar perigee, and is approximately 27.554,550 days in length. The anomalistic year is the average period of the revolution of the Earth around the Sun with respect to perihelion, and is approximately 365.259,6 days in length.

anomaly—As applied to astronomy, the anomaly is the angle made at any time by the radius vector of a planet or moon with its line of apsides, the angle being reckoned from perihelion or perigee in the direction of the body's motion. It is called the true anomaly when referred to the actual position of the body, and mean anomaly when referred to a fictitious body moving with a uniform angular velocity

1

equal to the average velocity of the real body and passing perihelion or perigee at the same time.

Antarctic Circumpolar Current—The largest permanent current in the world, setting eastward around the Antarctic Continent south of Cape Horn, Cape of Good Hope, Tasmania, and New Zealand. Through Drake Passage, it transports approximately 200×10^6 m^3/s. Same as West Wind Drift.

anticyclonic ring—A meander breaking off from the main oceanic current and spinning in a clockwise direction in the northern hemisphere (counter-clockwise in southern).

Antilles Current—A North Atlantic Ocean current setting northwestward along the northeast coasts of the Bahama Islands.

aphelion—The point in the orbit of the Earth (or other planet, etc.) farthest from the Sun.

apogean tides or tidal currents—Tides of decreased range or currents of decreased speed occurring monthly as the result of the Moon being in apogee. The apogean range (An) of the tide is the average range occurring at the time of apogean tides and is most conveniently computed from the harmonic constants. It is smaller than the mean range, where the type of tide is either semidiurnal or mixed, and is of no practical significance where the type of tide is predominantly diurnal.

apogee—The point in the orbit of the Moon or a man-made satellite farthest from the Earth. The point in the orbit of a satellite farthest from its companion body.

apparent secular trend—The nonperiodic tendency of sea level to rise, fall, or remain stationary with time. Technically, it is frequently defined as the slope of a least-squares line of regression through a relatively long series of yearly mean sea-level values. The word "apparent" is used since it is often not possible to know whether a trend is truly nonperiodic or merely a segment of a very long oscillation (relative to the length of the series).

apparent time—Time based upon the true position of the Sun as distinguished from mean time, which is measured by a fictitious Sun moving at a uniform rate. Apparent time is that shown by the sundial, and its noon is the time when the Sun crosses the meridian. The difference between apparent time and mean time is known as the equation of time. Although quite common many years ago, apparent time is seldom used now.

apsides—The points in the orbit of a planet or moon which are the nearest and farthest from the center of attraction. In the Earth's orbit these are called perihelion and aphelion, and in the Moon's orbit, perigee and apogee. The line passing through the apsides of an orbit is called the line of apsides.

argument—See equilibrium argument.

astres fictifs—Fictitious celestial bodies which are assumed to move in the celestial equator at uniform rates corresponding to the speeds of the several harmonic constituents of the tide producing force. Each astre fictif

crosses the meridian at a time corresponding to the maximum of the constituent that it represents.

astronomical day—See astronomical time.

astronomical tide—Same as tide.

astronomical time—Time formerly used in astronomical calculations in which the day began at noon rather than midnight. The astronomical day commenced at noon of the civil day of the same date. The hours of the day were numbered consecutively from zero (noon) to 23 (11 a.m. of the following morning). Up to the close of the year 1924, astronomical time was in general use in nautical almanacs. Beginning with the year 1925, the American Ephemeris and Nautical Almanac and similar publications of other countries abandoned the old astronomical time and adopted Greenwich civil (mean) time for the data given in their tables.

augmenting factor—A factor, used in connection with the harmonic analysis of tides or tidal currents by stencils, to allow for the fact that the tabulated hourly heights or speeds used in the summation for any constituent, other than S, do not in general occur on the exact constituent hours to which they are assigned, but may differ from the same by as much as a half hour.

automatic tide (water level) gauge—An instrument that automatically registers the rise and fall of the water level. In some instruments, the registration is accomplished by recording the heights at regular time intervals in digital format; in others, by a continuous graph of height against time.

azimuth—Azimuth of a body is the arc of the horizon intercepted between the north or south point and the foot of the vertical circle passing through the body. It is reckoned in degrees from either the north or south point clockwise entirely around the horizon. Azimuth of a current is the direction toward which it is flowing, and is usually reckoned from the north point.

B

baroclinic—The condition and type of motion when isobaric surfaces of a fluid are not parallel with isopycnal surfaces.

barotropic—The condition and type of motion when isobaric surfaces of a fluid are parallel with isopycnal surfaces.

barycenter—The common center of mass of the Sun-Earth System or the Moon-Earth System. The distance from the center of the Sun to the Sun-Earth barycenter is about 280 miles. The distance from the center of the Earth to the Moon-Earth barycenter is about 2,895 miles.

bench mark (BM)—A fixed physical object or mark used as reference for a horizontal or vertical datum. A tidal bench mark is one near a tide station to which the tide staff and tidal datums are referred. A primary bench mark is the principal mark of a group of tidal bench marks to which the tide staff and tidal datums are referred. The standard tidal bench mark of the National Ocean Service is a brass, bronze, or aluminum alloy disk 3-½ inches in diameter containing the inscription NATIONAL OCEAN SERVICE together with other individual identifying information. A geodetic bench mark identifies a surveyed point in the National Spatial Reference System. Bench mark disks of either type may, on occasion, serve simultaneously to reference both tidal and geodetic datums. Numerous bench marks of predecessor organizations to NOS, or parts of other organizations absorbed into NOS, still bear the inscriptions: U.S. COAST & GEODETIC SURVEY, NATIONAL GEODETIC SURVEY, NATIONAL OCEAN SURVEY, U.S. LAKE SURVEY, CORPS OF ENGINEERS, and U.S. ENGINEER OFFICE.

Benguela Current—A South Atlantic Ocean current setting northward along the southwest coast of Africa.

bore—Same as tidal bore.

Brazil Current—A South Atlantic Ocean current setting southwestward along the central coast of South America.

bubbler tide (water level) gauge—Same as gas purged pressure gauge.

C

California Current—A North Pacific Ocean current setting southeastward along the west coast of the United States and Baja California.

Callippic cycle—A period of four Metonic cycles equal to 76 Julian years, or 27,759 days. Devised by Callippus, a Greek astronomer, about 350 B.C., as a suggested improvement on the Metonic cycle for a period in which new and full Moon would recur on the same day of the year. Taking the length of the synodical month as 29.530,588 days, there are 940 lunations in the Callippic cycle, with about 0.25 day remaining.

Canary Current—A North Atlantic Ocean current setting southward off the west coast of Portugal and along the northwest coast of Africa.

celestial sphere—An imaginary sphere of infinite radius concentric with the Earth on which all celestial bodies except the Earth are imagined to be projected.

centibar—The unit of pressure equal to 1 metric ton (1000 kilograms) per meter per second per second. See decibar.

chart datum—The datum to which soundings on a chart are referred. It is usually taken to correspond to a low-water elevation, and its depression below mean sea level is represented by the symbol Z_o. Since 1980, chart datum has been implemented to mean lower low water for all marine waters of the United States, its territories, Commonwealth of Puerto Rico, and Trust Territory of the Pacific Islands. See datum and National Tidal Datum Convention of 1980.

Charybdis—Same as Galofaro.

chlorinity (Cl)—The total amount in grams of chlorine, bromine, and iodine contained in one kilogram of seawater, assuming the bromine and iodine to be replaced by chlorine. The number giving the chlorinity in grams per kilogram of a seawater sample is identical with the number giving the mass in grams of atomic weight silver just necessary to precipitate the halogens in 0.328,523,3 kilogram of the seawater sample.
$$S(‰) = 1.806,55 \times Cl(‰)$$
where $S(‰)$ is the salinity in parts per thousand. See salinity.

civil day—A mean solar day commencing at midnight.

civil time—Time in which the day begins at midnight as distinguished from the former astronomical time in which the day began at noon.

classification—See type of tide.

Coast and Geodetic Survey—A former name of the National Ocean Service. The organization was known as: Survey of the Coast from its founding in 1807 to 1836, Coast Survey from 1836 to 1878, Coast and Geodetic Survey from 1878 to 1970, and National Ocean Survey from 1970 to 1982. In 1982 it was named National Ocean Service. From 1965 to 1970, the Coast and Geodetic Survey was a component of the Environmental Science Services Administration (ESSA). The National Ocean Survey was a component of the National Oceanic and Atmospheric Administration (NOAA). NOAA became the successor to ESSA in 1970. The National Ocean Service is a component of NOAA, U.S. Department of Commerce.

coast line—The low water datum line for purposes of the Submerged Lands Act (Public Law 31). See shoreline.

coastal boundary—The mean high water line (MHWL) or mean higher high water line (MHHWL) when tidal lines are used as the coastal boundary. Also, lines used as boundaries inland of and measured from (or points thereon) the MHWL or MHHWL. See marine boundary.

coastal zone (legal definition for coastal zone management)—The term coastal zone means the coastal waters (including the lands therein and thereunder) and the adjacent shorelands (including the waters therein and thereunder), strongly influenced by each and in proximity to the shorelines of the several coastal states, and includes islands, transitional and intertidal areas, salt marshes, wetlands, and beaches. The zone extends, in Great Lakes waters, to the international boundary between the United States and Canada and in other areas seaward to the outer limit of the United States territorial sea. The zone extends inland from the shorelines only to the extent necessary to control shorelands, the uses of which have a direct and significant impact on the coastal waters. Excluded from the coastal zone are lands the use of which is by law subject solely to the discretion of or which is held in trust by the Federal Government, its officers, or agents.

coastline—Same as shoreline. See coast line.

cocurrent line—A line on a map or chart passing through places having the same current hour.

comparison of simultaneous observations—A reduction process in which a short series of tide or tidal current observations at any place is compared with simultaneous observations at a control station where tidal or tidal current constants have previously been determined from a long series of observations. The observations are typically high and low tides and monthly means. For tides, it is usually used to adjust constants from a subordinate station to the equivalent value that would be obtained from a 19-year series. See first reduction, standard method, modified-range ratio method, and direct method.

compass direction—Direction as indicated by compass without any correction for compass error. The direction indicated by a compass may differ by a considerable amount from true or magnetic direction.

compass error—The angular difference between a compass direction and the corresponding true direction. The compass error combines the effects of deviation and variation.

component—(1) Same as constituent. (2) That part of a tidal current velocity which, by resolution into orthogonal vectors, is found to flow in a specified direction.

compound tide—A harmonic tidal (or tidal current) constituent with a speed equal to the sum or difference of the speeds of two or more elementary constituents. The presence of compound tides is usually attributed to shallow water conditions.

constants, current—See current constants.

constants, harmonic—See harmonic constants.

constants, tidal—See tidal constants.

constituent—One of the harmonic elements in a mathematical expression for the tide-producing force and in corresponding formulas for the tide or tidal current. Each constituent represents a periodic change or variation in the relative positions of the Earth, Moon, and Sun. A single constituent is usually written in the form $y = A \cos(at + \alpha)$, in which y is a function of time as expressed by the symbol t and is reckoned from a specific origin. The coefficient A is called the amplitude of the constituent and is a measure of its relative importance. The angle $(at + \alpha)$ changes uniformly and its value at any time is called the phase of the constituent. The speed of the constituent is the rate of change in its phase and is represented by the symbol a in the formula. The quantity α is the phase of the constituent at the initial instant from which the time is reckoned. The period of the constituent is the time required for the phase to change through 360° and is the cycle of the astronomical condition represented by the constituent.

constituent day—The time of the rotation of the Earth with respect to a fictitious celestial body representing one of the periodic elements in the tidal forces. It approximates in length the lunar or solar day and corresponds to the period of a diurnal constituent or twice the period of a semidiurnal constituent. The term is not applicable to the long-period constituents.

constituent hour—One twenty-fourth part of a constituent day.

control current station—A current station at which continuous velocity observations have been made over a minimum period of 29 days. Its purpose is to provide data for computing accepted values of the harmonic and nonharmonic constants essential to tidal current predictions and circulatory studies. The data series from this station serves as the control for the reduction of relatively short series from subordinate current stations through the method of comparison of simultaneous observations. See current station and subordinate current station (1).

control station—See primary control tide station, secondary control tide station, and control current station.

corange line—A line passing through places of equal tidal range.

Coriolis force—A fictional force in the hydrodynamic equations of motion that takes into account the effect of the Earth's rotation on moving objects (including air and water) when viewed with reference to a coordinate system attached to the rotating Earth. The horizontal component is directed 90° to the right (when looking in the direction of motion) in the Northern Hemisphere and 90° to the left in the Southern. The horizontal component is zero at the Equator; also, when the object is at rest relative to the Earth. The Coriolis acceleration = $2v\Omega \sin ø$: where v is the speed of the object, Ω is the angular velocity of the Earth, and ø is the latitude. Named for Gaspard Gustave de Coriolis who published his formulation in 1835.

corrected current—A relatively short series of current observations from a subordinate station to which a factor is applied to adjust the current to a more representative value based on a relatively long series from a nearby control station. See current and total current.

cotidal hour—The average interval between the Moon's transit over the meridian of Greenwich and the time of the following high water at any place. This interval may be expressed either in solar or lunar time. When expressed in solar time, it is the same as the Greenwich high water interval. When expressed in lunar time, it is equal to the Greenwich high water interval multiplied by the factor 0.966.

cotidal line—A line on a chart or map passing through places having the same tidal hour.

countercurrent—A current usually setting in a direction opposite to that of a main current. See Equatorial Countercurrent.

crest—The highest point in a propagating wave. See high water and tidal wave.

current—Generally, a horizontal movement of water. Currents may be classified as tidal and nontidal. Tidal currents are caused by gravitational interactions between the Sun, Moon, and Earth and are part of the same general movement of the sea that is manifested in the vertical rise and fall, called tide. Tidal currents are periodic with a net velocity of zero over the particular tidal cycle. See tidal wave. Nontidal currents include the permanent currents in the general circulatory systems of the sea as well as temporary currents arising from more pronounced meteorological variability. Current, however, is also the British equivalent of our nontidal current. See total current.

current constants—Tidal current relations that remain practically constant for any particular locality. Current constants are classified as harmonic and nonharmonic. The harmonic constants consist of the amplitudes and epochs of the harmonic constituents, and the nonharmonic constants include the velocities and intervals derived directly from the current observations.

current curve—A graphic representation of the flow of the current. In the reversing type of tidal current, the curve is referred to rectangular coordinates with time represented by the abscissa and the speed of the current by the ordinate, the flood speeds being considered as positive and the ebb speeds as negative. In general, the current curve for a reversing tidal current approximates a cosine curve.

current diagram—A graphic table published in the Tidal Current Tables showing the speeds of the flood and ebb currents and the times of slacks and strengths over a considerable stretch of the channel of a tidal waterway, the times being referred to tide or tidal current phases at some reference station.

current difference—Difference between the time of slack water (or minimum current) or strength of current in any locality and the time of the corresponding phase of the tidal current at a reference station for which predictions are given in the Tidal Current Tables.

current direction—Same as set.

current ellipse—A graphic representation of a rotary current in which the velocity of the current at different hours of the tidal cycle is represented by radius vectors and vectoral angles. A line joining the extremities of the radius vectors will form a curve roughly approximating an ellipse. The cycle is completed in one-half tidal day or in a whole tidal day, according to whether the tidal current is of the semidiurnal or the diurnal type. A current of the mixed type will give a curve of two unequal loops each tidal day.

current hour—The mean interval between the transit of the Moon over the meridian of Greenwich and the time of strength of flood, modified by the times of slack water (or minimum current) and strength of ebb. In computing the mean current hour, an average is obtained of the intervals for the following phases: flood strength, slack (or minimum) before flood increased by 3.10 hours (one-fourth of tidal cycle), slack (or minimum) after flood decreased by 3.10 hours, and ebb strength increased or decreased by 6.21 hours (one-half of tidal cycle). Before taking the average, the four phases are made comparable by the addition or rejection of such multiples of 12.42 hours as may be necessary. The current hour is usually expressed in solar time, but if lunar time is desired, the solar hour should be multiplied by the factor 0.966.

current line—A graduated line attached to a current pole formerly used in measuring the velocity of the current. The line was marked in such a manner that the speed of the current, expressed in knots and tenths, was indicated directly by the length of line carried out by the current pole in a specified interval of time. When marked for a 60-second run, the principal divisions for whole knots were spaced at 101.33 feet and the subdivisions for tenths of knots were spaced at 10.13 feet. The current line was also known as a log line.

current meter—An instrument for measuring the speed and direction or just the speed of a current. The measurements are Eulerian when the meter is fixed or moored at a specific location. Current meters can be mechanical, electric, electromagnetic, acoustic, or any combination thereof.

current pole—A pole used in observing the velocity of the current. The pole formerly used by the Coast and Geodetic Survey was about 3 inches in diameter and 15 feet long, and was weighted at one end to float upright with the top about 1 foot out of water. Shorter poles were used when necessary for shallow water. In use, the pole was attached to the current line but separated from the graduated portion by an ungraded section of approximately 100 feet, known as the stray line. As the pole was carried out from an observing vessel by the current, the amount of line passing from the vessel during a specific time interval indicated the speed of the current. The set was obtained from a relative bearing from the vessel to the pole. The bearing was then related to the ship's compass and converted to true. See pelorus.

current station—The geographic location at which current observations are conducted. Also, the facilities used to make current observations. These may include a buoy, ground tackle, current meters, recording mechanism, and radio transmitter. See control current station and subordinate current station (1).

cyclonic ring—A meander breaking off from the main oceanic current and spinning in a counter-clockwise direction in the northern hemisphere (clockwise in southern).

D

data collection platform (DCP)—A microprocessor-based system that collects data from sensors, processes the data, stores the data in random access memory (RAM), and provides communication links for the retrieval or transmission of the data.

datum (vertical)—For marine applications, a base elevation used as a reference from which to reckon heights or depths. It is called a tidal datum when defined in terms of a certain phase of the tide. Tidal datums are local datums and should not be extended into areas which have differing hydrographic characteristics without substantiating measurements. In order that they may be recovered when needed, such datums are referenced to fixed points known as bench marks. See chart datum.

datum of tabulation—A permanent base elevation at a tide station to which all water level measurements are referred. The datum is unique to each station and is established at a lower elevation than the water is ever expected to reach. It is referenced to the primary bench mark at the station and is held constant regardless of changes to the water level gauge or tide staff. The datum of tabulation is most often at the zero of the first tide staff installed.

Davidson Current—A North Pacific Ocean counter-current setting northward between the California Current and the coasts of California, Oregon, and Washington during the winter months.

day—The period of rotation of the Earth. There are several kinds of days depending on whether the Sun, Moon, or other object or location is used as the reference for the rotation. See constituent day, lunar day, sidereal day, and solar day.

daylight saving time—A time used during the summer months, in some localities, in which clocks are advanced 1 hour from the usual standard time.

decibar—The practical unit for pressure in the ocean, equal to 10 centibars, and is the approximate pressure produced by each meter of overlying water

declination—Angular distance north or south of the celestial equator, taken as positive when north of the equator and negative when south. The Sun passes through its declinational cycle once a year, reaching its maximum north declination of approximately 23-½° about June 21 and its maximum south declination of approximately 23-½° about December 21. The Moon has an average declinational cycle of 27-½ days which is called a tropical month. Tides or tidal currents occurring near the times of maximum north or south declination of the Moon are called tropic tides or tropic currents, and those occurring when the Moon is over the Equator are called equatorial tides or equatorial currents. The maximum declination reached by the Moon in successive months depends upon the longitude of the Moon's node, and varies from 28-½° when the longitude of the ascending node is 0°, to 18-½° when the longitude of the node is 180°. The node cycle, or time required for the node to complete a circuit of 360° of longitude, is approximately 18.6 years. See epoch (2).

declinational inequality—Same as diurnal inequality.

declinational reduction—A processing of observed high and low waters or flood and ebb tidal currents to obtain quantities depending upon changes in the declination of the Moon; such as tropic ranges or speeds, height or speed inequalities, and tropic intervals.

density, in situ ($\rho_{s,t,p}$)—Mass per unit volume. The reciprocal of specific volume. In oceanography, the density of sea water, when expressed in gm/cm^3, is numerically equivalent to specific gravity and is a function of salinity, temperature, and pressure. See specific volume anomaly, thermosteric anomaly, sigma-t, and sigma-zero.

deviation (of compass)—The deflection of the needle of a magnetic compass due to masses of magnetic metal within a ship on which the compass is located. This deflection varies with different headings of the ship. The deviation is called easterly and marked plus if the deflection is to the right of magnetic north, and is called westerly and marked minus if it is to the left of magnetic north. A deviation table is a tabular arrangement showing the amount of deviation for different headings of the ship. Each compass requires a separate deviation table.

digital tide (water level) gauge—See automatic tide (water level) gauge.

direct method—A tidal datum computation method. Datums are determined directly by comparison with an appropriate control, for the available part of the tidal cycle. It is usually used only when a full range of tidal values are not available. For example: Direct Mean High Water, when low waters are not recorded.

direction of current—Same as set.

direction of wind—Direction from which the wind is blowing.

diurnal—Having a period or cycle of approximately one tidal day. Thus, the tide is said to be diurnal when only one high water and one low water occur during a tidal day, and the tidal current is said to be diurnal when there is a single flood and a single ebb period of a reversing current in the tidal day. A rotary current is diurnal if it changes its direction through all points of the compass once each tidal day. A diurnal constituent is one which has a single period in the constituent day. The symbol for such a constituent is the subscript 1. See stationary wave theory and type of tide.

diurnal inequality—The difference in height of the two high waters or of the two low waters of each tidal day; also, the difference in speed between the two flood tidal currents or the two ebb currents of each tidal day. The difference changes with the declination of the Moon and, to a lesser extent, with the declination of the Sun. In general, the inequality tends to increase with increasing declination, either north or south, and to diminish as the Moon approaches the Equator. Mean diurnal high water inequality (DHQ) is one-half the average difference between the two high waters of each tidal day observed over the National Tidal Datum Epoch. It is obtained by subtracting the mean of all the high waters from the mean of the higher high waters. Mean diurnal low water inequality (DLQ) is one-half the average difference between the two low waters of each tidal day observed over the National Tidal Datum Epoch. It is obtained by subtracting the mean of the lower low waters from the mean of all the low waters. Tropic high water inequality (HWQ) is the average difference between the two high waters of each tidal day at the times of tropic tides. Tropic low water inequality (LWQ) is the average difference between the two low waters of each tidal day at the times of tropic tides. Mean and tropic inequalities, as defined above, are applicable only when the type of tide is either semidiurnal or mixed. Diurnal inequality is sometimes called declinational inequality.

diurnal range—Same as great diurnal range.

diurnal tide level—A tidal datum midway between mean higher high water and mean lower low water.

double ebb—An ebb tidal current having two maxima of speed separated by a smaller ebb speed.

double flood—A flood tidal current having two maxima of speed separated by a smaller flood speed.

double tide—A double-headed tide, that is, a high water consisting of two maxima of nearly the same height separated by a relatively small depression, or a low water consisting of two minima separated by a relatively small elevation. Sometimes called an agger. See gulder.

drift (of current)—The speed of the current.

drift current—Same as wind drift.

duration of flood and duration of ebb—Duration of flood is the interval of time in which a tidal current is flooding, and duration of ebb is the interval in which it is ebbing, these intervals being reckoned from the middle of the intervening slack waters or minimum currents. Together they cover, on an average, a period of 12.42 hours for a semidiurnal tidal current or a period of 24.84 hours for a diurnal current. In a normal semidiurnal tidal current, the duration of flood and duration of ebb each will be approximately equal to 6.21 hours, but the times may be modified greatly by the presence of nontidal flow. In a river the duration of ebb is usually longer than the duration of flood because of fresh water discharge, especially during spring months when snow and ice melt are predominant influences.

duration of rise and duration of fall—Duration of rise is the interval from low water to high water, and duration of fall is the interval from high water to low water. Together they cover, on an average, a period of 12.42 hours for a semidiurnal tide or a period of 24.84 hours for a diurnal tide. In a normal semidiurnal tide, duration of rise and duration of fall each will be approximately equal to 6.21 hours, but in shallow waters and in rivers there is a tendency for a decrease in duration of rise and a corresponding increase in duration of fall.

dynamic decimeter—See geopotential as preferred term.

dynamic depth (height)—See geopotential difference as preferred term.

dynamic depth (height) anomaly—See geopotential anomaly as preferred term.

dynamic meter (D)—The former practical unit for geopotential difference (dynamic depth), equal to 10 geopotentials (dynamic decimeters). See geopotential (dynamic depth) anomaly.

dynamic topography—See geopotential topography as preferred term.

E

eagre (eager)—Same as tidal bore.

earth tide—Periodic movement of the Earth's crust caused by gravitational interactions between the Sun, Moon, and Earth.

East Africa Coast Current—Same as Somali Current.

East Australian Current—A South Pacific Ocean current setting southward along the east coast of Australia.

East Greenland Current—A North Atlantic Ocean current setting southward and then southwestward along the east coast of Greenland.

ebb axis—Average set of the current at ebb strength.

ebb current (ebb)—The movement of a tidal current away from shore or down a tidal river or estuary. In the mixed type of reversing tidal current, the terms greater ebb and lesser ebb are applied respectively to ebb tidal currents of greater and lesser speed each day. The terms maximum ebb and minimum ebb are applied to the maximum and minimum speeds of a current running continuously ebb, the speed alternately increasing and decreasing without coming to a slack or reversing. The expression maximum ebb is also applicable to any ebb current at the time of greatest speed. See ebb strength.

ebb interval—The interval between the transit of the Moon over the meridian of a place and the time of the following ebb strength.

ebb strength (strength of ebb)—Phase of the ebb tidal current at the time of maximum speed. Also, the speed at this time. See strength of current.

eccentricity of orbit—Ratio of the distance from the center to the focus of an elliptical orbit to the length of the semimajor axis. The eccentricity of orbit = $\sqrt{1 - (B / A)^2}$: where A and B are respectively the semimajor and semiminor axes of the orbit.

ecliptic—The intersection of the plane of the Earth's orbit with the celestial sphere.

eddy—A quasi-circular movement of water whose area is relatively small in comparison to the current with which it is associated.

edge waves—Waves moving between zones of high and low breakers along the shoreline. Edge waves contribute to changes in water level along the shoreface which helps to control the spacing of rip currents. See longshore current and rip current.

Ekman spiral—A logarithmic spiral (when projected on a horizontal plane) formed by the heads of current velocity vectors at increasing depths. The current vectors become progressively smaller with depth. They spiral to the right (looking in the direction of flow) in the Northern Hemisphere and to the left in the Southern with increasing depth. Theoretically, in deep water, the surface current vector sets 45° and the total mass transport sets 90° from the direction toward which the wind is blowing. Flow opposite to the surface current occurs at the so-called "depth of frictional resistance". The phenomenon occurs in wind drift currents in which only the Coriolis and frictional forces are significant. Named for Vagn Walfrid Ekman who, assuming a constant eddy viscosity, steady wind stress, and unlimited water depth and extent, derived the effect in 1905.

electric tape gauge—A gauge consisting of a graduated Monel metal tape on a metal reel (with supporting frame), voltmeter, and battery. Heights can be measured directly by unreeling the tape into its stilling well. When contact is made with the water's surface, the circuit is completed and the voltmeter needle moves. At that moment the length of tape is read against an index mark, the mark having a known elevation relative to the bench marks.

elimination—One of the final processes in the harmonic analysis of tides in which preliminary values for the harmonic constants of a number of constituents are cleared of the residual effects of each other.

epoch—(1) Also known as phase lag. Angular retardation of the maximum of a constituent of the observed tide (or tidal current) behind the corresponding maximum of the same constituent of the theoretical equilibrium tide. It may also be defined as the phase difference between a tidal constituent and its equilibrium argument. As referred to the local equilibrium argument, its symbol is κ. When referred to the corresponding Greenwich equilibrium argument, it is called the Greenwich epoch and is represented by G. A Greenwich epoch that has been modified to adjust to a particular time meridian for convenience in the prediction of tides is represented by g or by κ'. The relations between these epochs may be expressed by the following formula:

$$G = \kappa + pL$$
$$g = \kappa' = G - aS / 15$$

in which L is the longitude of the place and S is the longitude of the time meridian, these being taken as positive for west longitude and negative for east longitude; p is the number of constituent periods in the constituent day and is equal to 0 for all long-period constituents, 1 for diurnal constituents, 2 for semidiurnal constituents, and so forth; and a is the hourly speed of the constituent, all angular measurements being expressed in degrees. (2) As used in tidal datum determination, it is a 19-year cycle over which tidal height observations are meaned in order to establish the various datums. As there are periodic and apparent secular trends in sea level, a specific 19-year cycle (the National Tidal Datum Epoch) is selected so that all tidal datum determinations throughout the United States, its territories, Commonwealth of Puerto Rico, and Trust Territory of the Pacific Islands, will have a common reference. See National Tidal Datum Epoch.

equation of time— Difference between mean and apparent time. From the beginning of the year until near the middle of April, mean time is ahead of apparent time, the difference reaching a maximum of about 15 minutes near the middle of February. From the middle of April to the middle of June, mean time is behind apparent time but the difference is less than 5 minutes. From the middle of June to the first part of September, mean time is again ahead of apparent time with maximum difference less than 7 minutes. From the first of September until the later part of December, mean time is again behind apparent time, the difference reaching a maximum of nearly 17 minutes in the early part of November. The equation of time for each day in the year is given in the American Ephemeris and Nautical Almanac.

Equatorial Countercurrent—A current setting eastward between the North and South Equatorial Currents of the Atlantic, Pacific, and Indian (in northern winter) Oceans. In the Atlantic and Pacific, its axis lies about latitude 7° north and in the Indian, about 7° south.

equatorial tidal currents—Tidal currents occurring semimonthly as a result of the Moon being over the Equator. At these times the tendency of the Moon to produce a diurnal inequality in the tidal current is at a minimum.

equatorial tides—Tides occurring semimonthly as a result of the Moon being over the Equator. At these times the tendency of the Moon to produce a diurnal inequality in the tide is at a minimum.

Equatorial Undercurrent—A subsurface current setting eastward along the Equator in the Pacific, Atlantic, and Indian Oceans. In the Pacific, its core of maximum velocity lies at a depth of about 100 meters within the South Equatorial Current.

equilibrium argument—The theoretical phase of a constituent of the equilibrium tide. It is usually represented by the expression (V + u), in which V is a uniformly changing angular quantity involving multiples of the hour angle of the mean Sun, the mean longitudes of the Moon and Sun, and the mean longitude of lunar or solar perigee; and u is a slowly changing angle depending upon the longitude of the Moon's node. When pertaining to an initial instant of time, such as the beginning of a series of observations, it is expressed by $(V_o + u)$.

equilibrium theory—A model under which it is assumed that the waters covering the face of the Earth instantly respond to the tide-producing forces of the Moon and Sun to form a surface of equilibrium under the action of these forces. The model disregards friction, inertia, and the irregular distribution of the land masses of the Earth. The theoretical tide formed under these conditions is known as the equilibrium tide.

equilibrium tide—Hypothetical tide due to the tide producing forces under the equilibrium theory. Also known as gravitational tide.

equinoctial—The celestial equator.

equinoctial tides—Tides occurring near the times of the equinoxes.

equinoxes—The two points in the celestial sphere where the celestial equator intersects the ecliptic; also, the times when the Sun crosses the equator at these points. The vernal equinox is the point where the Sun crosses the Equator from south to north and it occurs about March 21. Celestial longitude is reckoned eastward from the vernal equinox. The autumnal equinox is the point where the Sun crosses the Equator from north to south and it occurs about September 23.

equipotential surface—Same as geopotential surface.

establishment of the port—Also known as high water, full and change (HWF&C). Average high water interval on days of the new and full Moon. This interval is also sometimes called the common or vulgar establishment to distinguish it from the corrected establishment, the latter being the mean of all the high water intervals. The latter is usually 10 to 15 minutes less than the common establishment.

estuary—An embayment of the coast in which fresh river water entering at its head mixes with the relatively saline ocean water. When tidal action is the dominant mixing agent it is usually termed a tidal estuary. Also, the lower reaches and mouth of a river emptying directly into the sea where tidal mixing takes place. The latter is sometimes called a river estuary.

Eulerian measurement—Observation of a current with a device fixed relative to the flow.

eustatic sea level rate—The worldwide change of sea level elevation with time. The changes are due to such causes as glacial melting or formation, thermal expansion or contraction of sea water, etc.

evection—A perturbation of the Moon depending upon the alternate increase and decrease of the eccentricity of its orbit, which is always a maximum when the Sun is passing the Moon's line of apsides and a minimum when the Sun is at right angles to it. The principal constituents in the tide resulting from the evectional inequality are ν_2, λ_2, and ρ_1.

extreme high water—The highest elevation reached by the sea as recorded by a water level gauge during a given period. The National Ocean Service routinely documents monthly and yearly extreme high waters for its control stations.

extreme low water—The lowest elevation reached by the sea as recorded by a water level gauge during a given period. The National Ocean Service routinely documents monthly and yearly extreme low water for its control stations.

F

Falkland Current—A South Atlantic Ocean current setting northeastward along the east coast of Argentina.

first reduction—A method of determining high and low water heights, time intervals, and ranges from an arithmetic mean without adjustment to a long-term series through comparison of simultaneous observations.

float well—A stilling well in which the float of a float-actuated water level gauge operates. See stilling well.

flood axis—The average set of the tidal current at strength of flood.

flood current (flood)—The movement of a tidal current toward the shore or up a tidal river or estuary. In the mixed type of reversing current, the terms greater flood and lesser flood are applied respectively to the two flood currents of greater and lesser speed of each day. The expression maximum flood is applicable to any flood current at the time of greatest speed. See flood strength.

flood interval—The interval between the transit of the Moon over the meridian of a place and the time of the following flood strength.

flood strength (strength of flood)—Phase of the flood tidal current at the time of maximum speed. Also, the speed at this time. See strength of current.

Florida Current—A North Atlantic Ocean current setting northward along the south-east coast of the United States. A segment of the Gulf Stream System, the Florida Current extends from the Straits of Florida to the region off Cape Hatteras.

flow—The British equivalent of the United States total current. Flow is the combination of tidal stream and current.

flushing time—The time required to remove or reduce (to a permissible concentration) any dissolved or suspended contaminant in an estuary or harbor.

forced wave—A wave generated and maintained by a continuous force.

fortnight—The time elapsed between the new and full moons. Half a synodical month or 14.765,294 days. See synodical month.

Fourier series—A series proposed by the French mathematician Fourier about the year 1807. The series involves the sines and cosines of whole multiples of a varying angle and is usually written in the following form:
$$y = A_\circ + A_1 \sin x + A_2 \sin 2x + A_3 \sin 3x + \ldots B_1 \cos x + B_2 \cos 2x + B_3 \cos 3x + \ldots$$
By taking a sufficient number of terms the series may be assumed to represent any periodic function of x.

free wave—A wave that continues to exist after the generating force has ceased to act. See gravity wave.

G

gage—See tide (water level) gauge.

Galofaro—A whirlpool in the Strait of Messina; at one time called Charybdis.

gas purged pressure gauge—A type of water level gauge in which gas, usually nitrogen, is emitted from a submerged orifice at a constant rate. Fluctuations in hydrostatic pressure due to changes in water level modify the recorded emission rate. Same as bubbler tide (water level) gauge.

gauge—See tide (water level) gauge.

geodetic datum—See National Geodetic Vertical Datum of 1929 (NGVD 1929) and North American Vertical Datum of 1988 (NAVD 1988).

geopotential—The unit of geopotential difference, equal to the gravity potential of 1 meter squared per second squared, m^2 / s^2, or 1 joule per kilogram, J / kg.

geopotential anomaly (ΔD)—The excess in geopotential difference over the standard geopotential difference [at a standard specific volume at 35 parts per thousand (‰) and 0 degrees C] between isobaric surfaces. See geopotential and geopotential topography.

$$\Delta D = \int_{P_1}^{P_2} \delta dp$$

where p is the pressure and δ, the specific volume anomaly. P_1 and P_2 are the pressures at the two surfaces.

geopotential difference—The work per unit mass gained or required in moving a unit mass vertically from one geopotential surface to another. See geopotential, geopotential anomaly, and geopotential topography.

geopotential (equipotential) surface—A surface that is everywhere normal to the acceleration of gravity.

geopotential topography—The topography of an equiscalar (usually isobaric) surface in terms of geopotential difference. As depicted on maps, isopleths are formed by the intersection of the isobaric surface with a series of geopotential surfaces. Thus, the field of isopleths represents variations in the geopotential anomaly of the isobaric surface above a chosen reference isobaric surface (such as a level of no motion).

geostrophic flow—A solution of the relative hydrodynamic equations of motion in which it is assumed that the horizontal component of the Coriolis force is balanced by the horizontal component of the pressure gradient force.

gradient flow—A solution of the relative hydrodynamic equations of motion in which only the horizontal Coriolis, pressure gradient, and centrifugal forces are considered.

gravitational tide—Same as equilibrium tide.

gravity wave—A wave for which the restoring force is gravity.

great diurnal range (Gt)—The difference in height between mean higher high water and mean lower low water. The expression may also be used in its contracted form, diurnal range.

great tropic range (Gc)—The difference in height between tropic higher high water and tropic lower low water. The expression may also be used in its contracted form, tropic range.

Greenwich argument—Equilibrium argument computed for the meridian of Greenwich.

Greenwich epoch—See epoch (1).

Greenwich interval—An interval referred to the transit of the Moon over the meridian of Greenwich, as distinguished from the local interval which is referred to the Moon's transit over the local meridian. The relation in hours between Greenwich and local intervals may be expressed by the formula:

Greenwich interval = local interval + 0.069L

where L is the west longitude of the local meridian in degrees. For east longitude, L is to be considered negative.

Gregorian calendar—The modern calendar in which every year divisible by 4 (excepting century years) and every century year divisible by 400 are bissextile (or leap) years with 366 days. All other years are common years with 365 days. The average length of this year is, therefore, 365.242,5 days which agrees very closely with the length of the tropical year (the period of changes in seasons). The Gregorian calendar was introduced by Pope Gregory in 1582, and immediately adopted by the Catholic countries in place of the Julian calendar previously in use. In making the change it was ordered that the day following October 4, 1582, of the Julian calendar be designated October 15, 1582, of the Gregorian calendar; the 10 days being dropped in order that the vernal equinox would fall on March 21. The Gregorian calendar was not adopted by England until 1752, but is now in general use throughout the world.

Guiana Current—An Atlantic Ocean current setting northwestward along the north-east coast of South America.

Guinea Current—An Atlantic Ocean current setting eastward along the west central coast of Africa. A continuation of the Equatorial Counter Current of the Atlantic Ocean.

gulder—Local name given to the double low water occurring on the south coast of England. See double tide.

Gulf Coast Low Water Datum (GCLWD)—A tidal datum. Used as chart datum from November 14, 1977, to November 27, 1980, for the coastal waters of the Gulf coast of the United States. GCLWD is defined as mean lower low water when the type of tide is mixed and mean low water (now mean lower low water) when the type of tide is diurnal. See National Tidal Datum Convention of 1980.

Gulf Coast Low Water Datum line—The line on a chart or map which represents the intersection of the land with the water surface at the elevation of Gulf Coast Low Water Datum.

Gulf Stream—A North Atlantic Ocean current setting northeastward off the east coast of the United States. A segment of the Gulf Stream System, the Gulf Stream extends from the region off Cape Hatteras to an area southeast of the Grand Banks at about latitude 40° north, longitude 50° west. It continues the flow of the Florida Current to the North Atlantic Current.

Gulf Stream System—The continuous current system composed of the Florida Current, Gulf Stream, and North Atlantic Current.

H

h—Rate of change (as of January 1, 1900) in mean longitude of the Sun.
h = 0.041,068,64° per solar hour.

half-tide level—Same as mean tide level.

halocline—A layer in which the salinity changes significantly (relative to the layers above and below) with depth.

harmonic analysis—The mathematical process by which the observed tide or tidal current at any place is separated into basic harmonic constituents.

harmonic analyzer—A machine designed for the resolution of a periodic curve into its harmonic constituents. Now performed by electronic digital computer.

harmonic constants—The amplitudes and epochs of the harmonic constituents of the tide or tidal current at any place.

harmonic constituent—See constituent.

harmonic function—In its simplest form, a quantity that varies as the cosine of an angle that increases uniformly with time. It may be expressed by the formula:

$y = A \cos at$

in which y is a function of time (t), A is a constant coefficient, and a is the rate of change in the angle at.

harmonic prediction—Method of predicting tides and tidal currents by combining the harmonic constituents into a single tide curve. The work is usually performed by electronic digital computer.

harmonic reduction—Same as harmonic analysis.

harmonic tide plane—Same as Indian spring low water.

head—The difference in water level at either end of a strait, channel, inlet, etc.

head of tide—The inland or upstream limit of water affected by the tide. For practical application in the tabulation for computation of tidal datums, head of tide is the inland or upstream point where the mean range becomes less than 0.2 foot. Tidal datums (except for mean water level) are not computed beyond head of tide.

high tide—Same as high water.

high water (HW)—The maximum height reached by a rising tide. The high water is due to the periodic tidal forces and the effects of meteorological, hydrologic, and/or oceanographic conditions. For tidal datum computational purposes, the maximum height is not considered a high water unless it contains a tidal high water.

high water, full and change (HWF&C)—Same as establishment of the port.

high water inequality—See diurnal inequality.

high water interval (HWI)—See lunitidal interval.

high water line—The intersection of the land with the water surface at an elevation of high water.

high water mark—A line or mark left upon tide flats, beach, or along shore objects indicating the elevation of the intrusion of high water. The mark may be a line of oil or scum on along shore objects, or a more or less continuous deposit of fine shell or debris on the foreshore or berm. This mark is physical evidence of the general height reached by wave run up at recent high waters. It should not be confused with the mean high water line or mean higher high water line.

higher high water (HHW)—The highest of the high waters (or single high water) of any specified tidal day due to the declinational effects of the Moon and Sun.

higher low water (HLW)—The highest of the low waters of any specified tidal day due to the declinational effects of the Moon and Sun.

Humboldt Current—Same as Peru Current.

hydraulic current—A current in a channel caused by a difference in the surface elevation at the two ends. Such a current may be expected in a strait connecting two bodies of water in which the tides differ in time or range. The current in the East River, New York, connecting Long Island Sound and New York Harbor, is an example.

hydrographic datum—A datum used for referencing depths of water and the heights of predicted tides or water level observations. Same as chart datum. See datum.

I

incremental shaft encoder—A component of a water level gauge for converting length to a shaft angle on a rotating disk. The position of the rotating disk is determined by single or dual optical or magnetic sensors to provide an electrical output. No electro-mechanical components or gears are used, so extremely low torque is required to move the float wheel, wire, and float mechanism.

Indian spring low water—A datum originated by Professor G. H. Darwin when investigating the tides of India. It is an elevation depressed below mean sea level by an amount equal to the sum of the amplitudes of he harmonic constituents M_2, S_2, K_1, and O_1.

Indian tide plane—Same as Indian spring low water.

inequality—A systematic departure from the mean value of a tidal quantity. See diurnal inequality, parallax inequality, and phase inequality.

inertial flow—A solution of the relative hydrodynamic equations of motion in which only the horizontal component of the Coriolis and centrifugal forces are balanced. This anticyclonic flow results from a sudden application and release of a driving force which then allows the system to continue on under its own momentum without further interference. The period of rotation is $2\pi / 2\Omega \sin \varnothing$, where $\Omega = 0.729{,}211 \times 10^{-4}$ radians s^{-1} and $\varnothing$ = latitude.

internal tide—A tidal wave propagating along a sharp density discontinuity, such as a thermocline, or in an area of gradually changing (vertically) density.

International Great Lakes Datum (1985) [IGLD 1985]—Mean water level at Rimouski/Pointe-au-Pere, Quebec, on the Gulf of St. Lawrence over the period 1970 through 1988, from which geopotential elevations (geopotential differences) throughout the Great Lakes region are measured. The term is often used to mean the entire system of geopotential elevations rather than just the referenced water level. See low water datum (1).

International Hydrographic Organization (formerly Bureau)—An institution consisting of representatives of a number of nations organized for the purpose of coordinating the hydrographic work of the participating governments. It had its origin in the International Hydrographic Conference in London in 1919. It has permanent headquarters in the Principality of Monaco and is supported by funds provided by the member nations. Its principal publications include the Hydrographic Review and special publications on technical subjects.

intertidal zone—(technical definition) The zone between the mean higher high water and mean lower low water lines.

interval—See lunitidal interval and lunicurrent interval.

inverse barometer effect—The inverse response of sea level to changes in atmospheric pressure. A static reduction of 1.005 mb in atmospheric pressure will cause a stationary rise of 1 cm in sea level.

Irminger Current—A North Atlantic Ocean current setting westward off the south-west coast of Iceland.

isanostere—An isopleth of either specific volume anomaly or thermosteric anomaly.

isobar—An isopleth of pressure.

isobaric surface—A surface of constant or uniform pressure.

isohaline—An isopleth of salinity. Constant or uniform in salinity.

isopleth—A line of constant or uniform value of a given quantity. See isanostere, isobar, isohaline, isopycnic, and isotherm.

isopycnic—An isopleth of density. Constant or uniform in density.

isotherm—An isopleth of temperature.

J

J_1—Smaller lunar elliptic diurnal constituent. This constituent, with M_1, modulates the amplitudes of the declinational K_1, for the effect of the Moon's elliptical orbit.
Speed = $T + s + h - p$ = 15.585,443,3° per solar hour.

Japan Current—Same as Kuroshio.

Julian calendar—A calendar introduced by Julius Caesar in the year 45 B.C., and slightly modified by Augustus a few years later. This calendar provided that the common year should consist of 365 days and that every fourth year, now known as a bissextile or leap year, should contain 366 days, making the average length of the year 365.25 days. It differs from the modern or Gregorian calendar in having every fourth year a leap year, while in the modern calendar century years not divisible by 400 are common years. See Gregorian calendar.

Julian date—Technique for the identification of successive days of the year when monthly notation is not desired. This is especially applicable in computer data processing and acquisition where indexing is necessary.

K

K_1—Lunisolar diurnal constituent. This constituent, with O_1, expresses the effect of the Moon's declination.

They account for diurnal inequality and, at extremes, diurnal tides. With P_1, it expresses the effect of the Sun's declination.
Speed = $T + h$ = 15.041,068,6° per solar hour.

K_2—Lunisolar semi diurnal constituent. This constituent modulates the amplitude and frequency of M_2 and S_2 for the declinational effect of the Moon and Sun, respectively.
Speed = $2T + 2h$ = 30.082,137,3° per solar hour.

kappa (κ)—Name of Greek letter used as the symbol for a constituent phase lag or epoch when referred to the local equilibrium argument and frequently taken to mean the same as local epoch. See epoch (1).

kappa prime (κ')— Name of Greek letter (with prime mark) used as the symbol for a constituent phase lag or epoch when the Greenwich equilibrium argument (G) has been modified to a particular time meridian. Same as g. See kappa (κ) and epoch (1).

knot—A speed unit of 1 international nautical mile (1,852.0 meters or 6,076.115,49 international feet) per hour.

Kuroshio—"Black Stream" in Japanese. A North Pacific Ocean current setting northeastward off the east coast of Taiwan and Japan from Taiwan to about latitude 35° north.

Kuroshio Extension—A North Pacific Ocean current setting eastward from about longitude 145° east to about 160° east. It continues the flow of the Kuroshio to the North Pacific Current.

Kuroshio System—The current system composed of the Kuroshio, Tsushima Current, Kuroshio Extension, and North Pacific Current.

L

L_2—Smaller lunar elliptic semi diurnal constituent. This constituent, with N_2, modulates the amplitude and frequency of M_2 for the effect of variation in the Moon's orbital speed due to its elliptical orbit.
Speed = $2T - s + 2h - p$ = 29.528,478,9° per solar hour.

Labrador Current—A North Atlantic Ocean current setting southeastward along the east coasts of Baffin Island, Labrador, and Newfoundland.

lagging of tide—The periodic retardation in the time of occurrence of high and low water due to changes in the relative positions of the Moon and Sun.

Lagrangian measurement—Observation of a current with a device moving with the current.

lambda (λ_2)—Smaller lunar evectional constituent. This constituent, with ν_2, μ_2, and (S_2), modulates the amplitude and frequency of M_2 for the effects of variation in solar attraction of the Moon. This attraction results in a slight pear-shaped lunar ellipse and a difference in lunar orbital speed between motion toward and away from the Sun. Although (S_2) has the same speed as S_2, its amplitude is extremely small.
Speed = $2T - s + p$ = 29.455,625,3° per solar hour.

latitude—The angular distance between a terrestrial position and the equator measured northward or southward from the equator along a meridian of longitude.

leap year—A calendar year containing 366 days. According to the present Gregorian calendar, all years with the date-number divisible by 4 are leap years, except century years. The latter are leap years when the date-number is divisible by 400.

level of no motion—A level (or layer) at which it is assumed that an isobaric surface coincides with a geopotential surface. A level (or layer) at which there is no horizontal pressure gradient force.

level surface—See geopotential surface as preferred term.

littoral current—A current in the littoral zone such as a long shore or rip current.

littoral zone—In coastal engineering, the area from the shoreline to just beyond the breaker zone. In biological oceanography, it is that part of the benthic division extending from the high water line out to a depth of about 200 meters. The littoral system is divided into a eulittoral and sublittoral zone, separated at a depth of about 50 meters. Also, frequently used interchangeably with intertidal zone.

local epoch—See kappa (κ) and epoch (1).

local time—Time in which noon is defined by the transit of the Sun over the local meridian as distinguished from standard time which is based upon the transit of the Sun over a standard meridian. Local time may be either mean or apparent, according to whether reference is to the mean or actual Sun. Local time was in general use in the United States until 1883, when standard time was adopted. The use of local time in other parts of the world has also been practically abandoned in favor of the more convenient standard time.

log line—A graduated line used to measure the speed of a vessel through the water or to measure the velocity of the current from a vessel at anchor. See current line.

long period constituent—A tidal or tidal current constituent with a period that is independent of the rotation of the Earth but which depends upon the orbital movement of the Moon or the Earth. The principal lunar long period constituents have periods approximating a month and half a month, and the principal solar long period constituents have periods approximating a year and half a year.

long period waves (long waves)—Forced or free waves whose lengths are much longer than the water depth. See tidal wave and tsunami.

longitude—Angular distance along a great circle of reference reckoned from an accepted origin to the projection of any point on that circle. Longitude on the Earth's surface is measured on the Equator east and west of the meridian of Greenwich and may be expressed either in degrees or in hours, the hour being taken as the equivalent of 15° of longitude. Celestial longitude is measured in the ecliptic eastward from the vernal equinox. The mean longitude of a celestial body moving in an orbit is the longitude that would be attained by a point moving uniformly in the circle of reference at the same average angular velocity as that of the body, with the initial position of the point so taken that its longitude would be the same as that of the body at a certain specified position in its orbit. With a common initial point, the mean longitude of a body will be the same in whatever circle it may be reckoned.

longshore current—A current paralleling the shore largely within the surf zone. It is caused by the excess water brought to the zone by the small net mass transport of wind waves. Long shore currents feed into rip currents. See progressive wave.

loop of stationary wave—That portion of the oscillating area where the vertical movement is greatest.

Loop Current—A current setting clockwise in the Gulf of Mexico. It enters through the Yucatan Channel from the Caribbean Sea and leaves through the Straits of Florida.

low tide—Same as low water.

low water (LW)—The minimum height reached by a falling tide. The low water is due to the periodic tidal forces and the effects of meteorological, hydrologic, and/or oceanographic conditions. For tidal datum computational purposes, the minimum height is not considered a low water unless it contains a tidal low water.

low water datum (LWD)—(1) The geopotential elevation (geopotential difference) for each of the Great Lakes and Lake St. Clair and the corresponding sloping surfaces of the St. Marys, St. Clair, Detroit, Niagara, and St. Lawrence Rivers to which are referred the depths shown on the navigational charts and the authorized depths for navigation improvement projects. Elevations of these planes are referred to IGLD 1985 and are Lake Superior—183.2 meters, Lakes Michigan and Huron—176.0 meters, Lake St. Clair—174.4 meters, Lake Erie—173.5 meters, and Lake Ontario—74.2 meters. (2) An approximation of mean low water that has been adopted as a standard reference for a limited area and is retained for an indefinite period regardless of the fact that it may differ slightly from a better determination of mean low water from a subsequent series of observations. Used primarily for river and harbor engineering purposes. Boston low water datum is an example.

low water equinoctial springs—Low water springs near the times of the equinoxes. Expressed in terms of the harmonic constants, it is an elevation depressed below mean sea level by an amount equal to the sum of the amplitudes of the constituents M_2, S_2, and K_2.

low water inequality—See diurnal inequality.

low water interval (LWI)—See lunitidal interval.

low water line—The intersection of the land with the water surface at an elevation of low water.

lower high water (LHW)—The lowest of the high waters of any specified tidal day due to the declinational effects of the Moon and Sun.

lower low water (LLW)—The lowest of the low waters (or single low water) of any specified tidal day due to the declinational effects of the Moon and Sun.

lower low water datum (LLWD)—An approximation of mean lower low water that has been adopted as a standard reference for a limited area and is retained for an indefinite period regardless of the fact that it may differ slightly from a better determination of mean lower low water from a subsequent series of observations. Used primarily for river and harbor engineering purposes. Columbia River lower low water datum is an example.

lowest astronomical tide—As defined by the International Hydrographic Organization, the lowest tide level that can be predicted to occur under average meteorological conditions and under any combination of astronomical conditions.

lunar cycle—An ambiguous expression which has been applied to various cycles associated with the Moon's motion. See Callippic cycle, Metonic cycle, node cycle, and synodical month.

lunar day—The time of the rotation of the Earth with respect to the Moon, or the interval between two successive upper transits of the Moon over the meridian of a place. The mean lunar day is approximately 24.84 solar hours in length, or 1.035 times as great as the mean solar day.

lunar interval—The difference in time between the transit of the Moon over the meridian of Greenwich and a local meridian. The average value of this interval, expressed in hours, is 0.069 L, where L is the local longitude in degrees, positive for west longitude and negative for east. The lunar interval equals the difference between the local and Greenwich interval of a tide or current phase.

lunar month—Same as synodical month.

lunar nodes—The points where the plane of the Moon's orbit intersects the ecliptic. The point where the Moon crosses in going from south to north is called the ascending node and the point where the crossing is from north to south is called the descending node. References are usually made to the ascending node which, for brevity, may be called the node.

lunar tide—That part of the tide on the Earth due solely to the Moon as distinguished from that part due to the Sun.

lunar time—Time based upon the rotation of the Earth relative to the Moon. See lunar day.

lunation—Same as synodical month.

lunicurrent interval—The interval between the Moon's transit (upper or lower) over the local or Greenwich meridian and a specified phase of the tidal current following the transit. Examples are strength of flood interval and strength of ebb interval, which may be abbreviated to flood interval and ebb interval, respectively. The interval is described as local or Greenwich according

to whether the reference is to the Moon's transit over the local or Greenwich meridian. When not otherwise specified, the reference is assumed to be local. For a and b markings, see lunitidal interval.

lunisolar tides—Harmonic tidal constituents K_1, and K_2, which are derived partly from the development of the lunar tide and partly from the solar tide, the constituent speeds being the same in both cases. Also, the lunisolar synodic fortnightly constituent MSf.

lunitidal interval—The interval between the Moon's transit (upper or lower) over the local or Greenwich meridian and the following high or low water. The average of all high water intervals for all phases of the Moon is known as mean high water lunitidal interval and is abbreviated to high water interval (HWI). Similarly, mean low water lunitidal interval is abbreviated to low water interval (LWI). The interval is described as local or Greenwich according to whether the reference is to the transit over the local or Greenwich meridian. When not otherwise specified, the reference is assumed to be local. When there is considerable diurnal inequality in the tide, separate intervals may be obtained for the higher high waters, lower high waters, higher low waters, and lower low waters. These are designated respectively as higher high water interval (HHWI), lower high water interval (LHWI), higher low water interval (HLWI), and lower low water interval (LLWI). In such cases, and also when the tide is diurnal, it is necessary to distinguish between the upper and lower transit of the Moon with reference to its declination. Intervals referred to the Moon's upper transit at the time of its north declination or the lower transit at the time of south declination are marked a. Intervals referred to the Moon's lower transit at the time of its north declination or to the upper transit at the time of south declination are marked b.

M

M_1—Smaller lunar elliptic diurnal constituent. This constituent, with J_1, modulates the amplitude of the declinational K_1, for the effect of the Moon's elliptical orbit. A slightly slower constituent, designated (M_1), with Q_1, modulates the amplitude and frequency of the declinational O_1, for the same effect.

Speed = $T - s + h + p$ = 14.496,693,9° per solar hour.

M_2—Principal lunar semidiurnal constituent. This constituent represents the rotation of the Earth with respect to the Moon.

Speed = $2T - 2s + 2h$ = 28.984,104,2° per solar hour.

M_3—Lunar terdiurnal constituent. A shallow water compound constituent. See shallow water constituent.

Speed = $3T - 3s + 3h$ = 43.476,156,3° per solar hour.

M_4, M_6, M_8—Shallow water overtides of the principal lunar constituent. See shallow water constituent.

Speed of M_4 = $2M_2$ = $4T - 4s + 4h$ = 57.968,208,4° per solar hour.

Speed of $M_6 = 3M_2 = 6T - 6s + 6h = 86.952,312,7°$ per solar hour.

Speed of $M_8 = 4M_2 = 8T - 8s + 8h = 115.936,416,9°$ per solar hour.

Maelstrom—Famous whirlpool off the coast of Norway in the Lofoten Islands between Moskenesoy and Mosken.

magnetic azimuth—Azimuth reckoned from the magnetic north or magnetic south. See magnetic direction.

magnetic declination—Same as variation.

magnetic direction—Direction as indicated by a magnetic compass after correction for deviation but without correction for variation.

marigram—A graphic record of the rise and fall of water level. The record is in the form of a curve in which time is generally represented on the abscissa and the height of the water level on the ordinate. See tide curve.

marine boundary—The mean lower low water line (MLLWL) when used as a boundary. Also, lines used as boundaries seaward of and measured from (or points thereon) the MLLWL. See coastal boundary.

mascaret—French for tidal bore.

mean current hour—Same as current hour.

mean diurnal tide level (MDTL)—A tidal datum. The arithmetic mean of mean higher high water and mean lower low water.

mean high water (MHW)—A tidal datum. The average of all the high water heights observed over the National Tidal Datum Epoch. For stations with shorter series, comparison of simultaneous observations with a control tide station is made in order to derive the equivalent datum of the National Tidal Datum Epoch.

mean high water line (MHWL)—The line on a chart or map which represents the intersection of the land with the water surface at the elevation of mean high water. See shoreline.

mean higher high water (MHHW)—A tidal datum. The average of the higher high water height of each tidal day observed over the National Tidal Datum Epoch. For stations with shorter series, comparison of simultaneous observations with a control tide station is made in order to derive the equivalent datum of the National Tidal Datum Epoch.

mean higher high water line (MHHWL)—The line on a chart or map which represents the intersection of the land with the water surface at the elevation of mean higher high water.

mean low water (MLW)—A tidal datum. The average of all the low water heights observed over the National Tidal Datum Epoch. For stations with shorter series, comparison of simultaneous observations with a control tide station is made in order to derive the equivalent datum of the National Tidal Datum Epoch.

mean low water line (MLWL)—The line on a chart or map which represents the intersection of the land with the water surface at the elevation of mean low water.

mean low water springs (MLWS)—A tidal datum. Frequently abbreviated spring low water. The arithmetic mean of the low water heights occurring at the time of spring tides observed over the National Tidal Datum Epoch. It is usually derived by taking an elevation depressed below the half-tide level by an amount equal to one-half the spring range of tide, necessary corrections being applied to reduce the result to a mean value. This datum is used, to a considerable extent, for hydrographic work outside of the United States and is the level of reference for the Pacific approaches to the Panama Canal.

mean lower low water (MLLW)—A tidal datum. The average of the lower low water height of each tidal day observed over the National Tidal Datum Epoch. For stations with shorter series, comparison of simultaneous observations with a control tide station is made in order to derive the equivalent datum of the National Tidal Datum Epoch.

mean lower low water line (MLLWL)—The line on a chart or map which represents the intersection of the land with the water surface at the elevation of mean lower low water.

mean range of tide (Mn)—The difference in height between mean high water and mean low water.

mean rise—The height of mean high water above the elevation of chart datum.

mean rise interval (MRI)—The average interval between the transit of the Moon and the middle of the period of the rise of the tide. It may be computed by adding half the duration of rise to the mean low water interval, subtracting the semidiurnal tidal period of 12.42 hours when greater than this amount. The mean rise interval may be either local or Greenwich according to whether it is referred to the local or Greenwich transit.

mean river level—A tidal datum. The average height of the surface of a tidal river at any point for all stages of the tide observed over the National Tidal Datum Epoch. It is usually determined from hourly height readings. In rivers subject to occasional freshets, the river level may undergo wide variations and, for practical purposes, certain months of the year may be excluded in the determination of the tidal datum. For charting purposes, tidal datums for rivers are usually based on observations during selected periods when the river is at or near a low water stage.

mean sea level (MSL)—A tidal datum. The arithmetic mean of hourly heights observed over the National Tidal Datum Epoch. Shorter series are specified in the name; e.g., monthly mean sea level and yearly mean sea level.

mean sun—A fictitious sun which is assumed to move in the celestial equator at a uniform speed corresponding to the average angular speed of the real Sun in the ecliptic, the mean sun being alternately in advance and behind the real Sun. It is used as a reference for reckoning mean time, noon of mean local time corresponding to the time of the transit of the mean sun over the local meridian. See equation of time and mean time.

mean tide level (MTL)—A tidal datum. The arithmetic mean of mean high water and mean low water. Same as half-tide level.

mean time—Time based upon the hour angle of the mean sun as distinguished from apparent time which is based upon the position of the real Sun. The difference between apparent and mean time is known as the equation of time.

mean water level (MWL)—A datum. The mean surface elevation as determined by averaging the heights of the water at equal intervals of time, usually hourly. Mean water level is used in areas of little or no range in tide.

mean water level line (MWLL)—The line on a chart or map which represents the intersection of the land with the water surface at the elevation of mean water level.

meteorological tides—Tidal constituents having their origin in the daily or seasonal variations in weather conditions which may occur with some degree of periodicity. The principal meteorological constituents recognized in the tides are Sa, Ssa, and S_1. See storm surge.

Metonic cycle—A period of almost 19 years or 235 lunations. Devised by Meton, an Athenian astronomer who lived in the fifth century B.C., for the purpose of obtaining a period in which new and full Moon would recur on the same day of the year. Taking the Julian year of 365.25 days and the synodical month as 29.530,588 days, we have the 19-year period of 6,939.75 days as compared with the 235 lunations of 6,939.69 days, a difference of only 0.06 day.

Mf—Lunar fortnightly constituent. This constituent expresses the effect of departure from a sinusoidal declinational motion.
Speed = 2s = 1.098,033,1° per solar hour.

midextreme tide—An elevation midway between extreme high water and extreme low water occurring in any locality.

mixed (current)—Type of tidal current characterized by a conspicuous diurnal inequality in the greater and lesser flood strengths and/or greater and lesser ebb strengths. See flood current and ebb current.

mixed (tide)—Type of tide characterized by a conspicuous diurnal inequality in the higher high and lower high waters and/or higher low and lower low waters. See type of tide.

Mm—Lunar monthly constituent. This constituent expresses the effect of irregularities in the Moon's rate of change of distance and speed in orbit.
Speed = s – p = 0.544,374,7° per solar hour.

modified epoch—See kappa prime (κ') and epoch (1).

modified-range ratio method—A tidal datum computation method. Generally used for the East Coast, Gulf Coast, and Caribbean Island stations. Values needed are mean tide level (MTL), mean diurnal tide level (DTL), mean range of tide (MN), and great diurnal range (GT) as determined by comparison with an appropriate control. From those, the following are computed:
MLW = MTL - (0.5*MN)
MHW = MLW + MN
MLLW = DTL - (0.5*GT)
MHHW = MLLW + GT

Monsoon Current (Southwest Monsoon Current)—An Indian Ocean current setting in a generally eastward to southeastward direction off India and Ceylon. It replaces the North Equatorial Current, reversed by wind stress of the south-west monsoons, in August and September.

month—The period of the revolution of the Moon around the Earth. The month is designated as siderial, tropical, anomalistic, nodical, or synodical according to whether the revolution is relative to a fixed star, vernal equinox, perigee, ascending node, or Sun. The calendar month is a rough approximation to the synodical month.

MSf—Lunisolar synodic fortnightly constituent.
Speed = 2s – 2h = 1.015,895,8° per solar hour.

mu (μ_2)—Variational constituent. See lambda.
Speed = 2T – 4s + 4h = 27.968,208,4° per solar hour.

multiple tide staff—A succession of tide staffs on a sloping shore so placed that the vertical graduations on the several staffs will form a continuous scale referred to the same datum.

N

N—Rate of change (as of January 1, 1900) in mean longitude of the Moon's node.
N = – 0.002,206,41° per solar hour.

N_2—Larger lunar elliptic semi diurnal constituent. See L_2
Speed = 2T – 3s + 2h + p = 28.439,729,5° per solar hour.

$2N_2$—Lunar elliptic semi diurnal second-order constituent.
Speed = 2T – 4s + 2h + 2p = 27.895,354,8° per solar hour.

National Geodetic Vertical Datum of 1929 [NGVD 1929]—A fixed reference adopted as a standard geodetic datum for elevations determined by leveling. The datum was derived for surveys from a general adjustment of the first-order leveling nets of both the United States and Canada. In the adjustment, mean sea level was held fixed as observed at 21 tide stations in the United States and 5 in Canada. The year indicates the time of the general adjustment. A synonym for Sea-level Datum of 1929. The geodetic datum is fixed and does not take into account the changing stands of sea level. Because there are many variables affecting sea level, and because the geodetic datum represents a best fit over a broad area, the relationship between the geodetic datum and local mean sea level is not consistent from one location to another in either time or space. For this reason, the National Geodetic Vertical Datum should not be confused with mean sea level. See North American Vertical Datum of 1988 (NAVD 1988).

National Spatial Reference System (NSRS)—A consistent national coordinate system that defines latitude, longitude, height, scale, gravity, and orientation throughout the nation, and how these values change with time. The NSRS is developed and maintained by the National

Geodetic Survey using advanced geodetic, photogrammetric, and remote sensing techniques.

National Tidal Datum Convention of 1980—Effective November 28, 1980, the Convention: (1) establishes one uniform, continuous tidal datum system for all marine waters of the United States, its territories, Commonwealth of Puerto Rico, and Trust Territory of the Pacific Islands, for the first time in history; (2) provides a tidal datum system independent of computations based on type of tide; (3) lowers chart datum from mean low water to mean lower low water along the Atlantic coast of the United States; (4) updates the National Tidal Datum Epoch from 1941 through 1959, to 1960 through 1978; (5) changes the name Gulf Coast Low Water Datum to mean lower low water; (6) introduces the tidal datum of mean higher high water in areas of predominantly diurnal tides; and (7) lowers mean high water in areas of predominantly diurnal tides. See chart datum.

National Tidal Datum Epoch—The specific 19-year period adopted by the National Ocean Service as the official time segment over which tide observations are taken and reduced to obtain mean values (e.g., mean lower low water, etc.) for tidal datums. It is necessary for standardization because of periodic and apparent secular trends in sea level. The present National Tidal Datum Epoch is 1960 through 1978. It is reviewed annually for possible revision and must be actively considered for revision every 25 years.

National Water Level Observation Network (NWLON)—The network of tide and water level stations operated by the National Ocean Service along the marine and Great Lakes coasts and islands of the United States.

The NWLON is composed of the primary and secondary control tide stations of the National Ocean Service. This Network provides the basic tidal datums for coastal and marine boundaries and for chart datum of the United States. Tide observations at a secondary control tide station or tertiary tide station are reduced to equivalent 19-year tidal datums through comparison of simultaneous observations with a primary control tide station. In addition to hydrography, nautical charting, and delineation of coastal and marine boundaries, the Network is used for coastal processes and tectonic studies, tsunami and storm surge warnings, and climate monitoring.

The National Water Level Observation Network also includes stations operated throughout the Great Lakes Basin. The network supports regulation, navigation and charting, river and harbor improvement, power generation, various scientific activities, and the adjustment for vertical movement of the Earth's crust in the Great Lakes Basin.

neap range—See neap tides.

neap tides or tidal currents—Tides of decreased range or tidal currents of decreased speed occurring semimonthly as the result of the Moon being in quadrature. The neap range (Np) of the tide is the average range

occurring at the time of neap tides and is most conveniently computed from the harmonic constants. It is smaller than the mean range where the type of tide is either semidiurnal or mixed and is of no practical significance where the type of tide is predominantly diurnal. The average height of the high waters of the neap tide is called neap high water or high water neaps (MHWN) and the average height of the corresponding low waters is called neap low water or low water neaps (MLWN).

Next Generation Water Level Measurement System (NGWLMS)—A fully integrated system encompassing new technology sensors and recording equipment, multiple data transmission options, and an integrated data processing, analysis, and dissemination subsystem.

nodal line—A line in an oscillating body of water along which there is a minimum or zero rise and fall of the tide.

nodal point—The zero tide point in an amphidromic region.

node—See lunar nodes.

node cycle—Period of approximately 18.61 Julian years required for the regression of the Moon's nodes to complete a circuit of 360° of longitude. It is accompanied by a corresponding cycle of changing inclination of the Moon's orbit relative to the plane of the Earth's Equator, with resulting inequalities in the rise and fall of the tide and speed of the tidal current.

node factor (f)—A factor depending upon the longitude of the Moon's node which, when applied to the mean coefficient of a tidal constituent, will adapt the same to a particular year for which predictions are to be made.

nodical month—Average period of the revolution of the Moon around the Earth with respect to the Moon's ascending node. It is approximately 27.212,220 days in length.

nonharmonic constants—Tidal constants such as lunitidal intervals, ranges, and inequalities which may be derived directly from high and low water observations without regard to the harmonic constituents of the tide. Also applicable to tidal currents.

nontidal current—See current.

normal tide—A nontechnical term synonymous with tide; i.e., the rise and fall of the ocean due to the gravitational interactions of the Sun, Moon, and Earth alone. Use of this term is discouraged.

North American Vertical Datum of 1988 [NAVD 1988]—A fixed reference for elevations determined by geodetic leveling. The datum was derived from a general adjustment of the first-order terrestrial leveling nets of the United States, Canada, and Mexico. In the adjustment, only the height of the primary tidal bench mark, referenced to the International Great Lakes Datum of 1985 (IGLD 1985) local mean sea level height value, at Father Point, Rimouski, Quebec, Canada was held fixed, thus providing minimum constraint. NAVD 1988 and IGLD 1985 are not identical. However, NAVD 1988 bench mark values are given in Helmert orthometric height units while IGLD 1985 values are in dynamic heights. See International Great Lakes Datum of 1985, National Geodetic Vertical Datum of 1929, and geopotential difference.

North Atlantic Current—A North Atlantic Ocean current setting northeastward from southeast of the Grand Banks at about latitude 40° north, longitude 50° west, to the British Isles. A segment of the Gulf Stream System, the North Atlantic Current continues the flow of the Gulf Stream to the Norwegian and Canary Currents.

North Cape Current—An Arctic Ocean current setting eastward off the north coast of Scandinavia in the Barrents Sea.

North Equatorial Current—A current setting westward in the North Atlantic and North Pacific Oceans and in the Indian Ocean from about October to July. It occurs immediately north of the Equatorial Counter Current.

North Pacific Current—A North Pacific Ocean current setting eastward from about 160° east to somewhat beyond about 150° west. It continues the flow of the Kuroshio Extension, sending branches to the south.

Norwegian Current—A North Atlantic Ocean current setting northeastward off the coast of Norway.

nu (ν_2)—Larger lunar evectional constituent. See lambda.
Speed = $2T - 3s + 4h - p = 28.512,583,1°$ per solar hour.

O

O_1—Lunar diurnal constituent. See K_1.
Speed = $T - 2s + h = 13.943,035,6°$ per solar hour.

obliquity factor—A factor in an expression for a constituent tide (or tidal current) involving the angle of the inclination of the Moon's orbit to the plane of the Earth's Equator.

obliquity of the ecliptic—The angle which the ecliptic makes with the plane of the Earth's Equator. Its value is approximately 23.45°.

obliquity of the Moon's orbit—The angle which the Moon's orbit makes with the plane of the Earth's Equator. Its value varies from 18.3° to 28.6°, depending upon the longitude of the Moon's ascending node; the smaller value corresponding to a longitude of 180° and the larger one, to a longitude of 0°.

oceanography—Oceanography is the science of all aspects of the oceans, in spite of its etymology. The term, oceanography, implies the interrelationships of the various marine sciences of which it is composed. This connotation has arisen through the historical development of marine research in which it has been found that a true understanding of the oceans is best achieved through investigations based on the realization that water, its organic and inorganic contents, motions, and boundaries are mutually related and interdependent.

OO_1—Lunar diurnal, second-order, constituent.
Speed = $T + 2s + h = 16.139,101,7°$ per solar hour.

ordinary—With respect to tides, the use of this nontechnical word has, for the most part, been determined to be synonymous with mean. Thus, ordinary high (low) water is the equivalent of mean high (low) water. The use of ordinary in tidal terms is discouraged.

orifice—See stilling well and protective well.

overfalls—Breaking waves caused by the meeting of currents or by waves moving against the current. See rip.

overtide—A harmonic tidal (or tidal current) constituent with a speed that is an exact multiple of the speed of one of the fundamental constituents derived from the development of the tide-producing force. The presence of overtides is usually attributed to shallow water conditions. The overtides usually considered in tidal work are the harmonics of the principal lunar and solar semidiurnal constituents M_2 and S_2, and are designated by the symbols M_4, M_6, M_8, S_4, S_6, etc. The magnitudes of these harmonics relative to those of the fundamental constituents are usually greater in the tidal current than in the tide.

Oyashio—A current setting southwestward along the Siberian, Kamchatka, and Kuril Islands coasts in the Bering Sea and North Pacific Ocean.

P

p—Rate of change (as of January 1, 1900) in mean longitude of lunar perigee.
p = 0.004,641,83° per solar hour.

p_1—Rate of change (as of January 1, 1900) in mean longitude of solar perigee.
p_1 = 0.000,001,96° per solar hour.

P_1—Solar diurnal constituent. See K_1.
Speed = $T - h = 14.958,931,4°$ per solar hour.

parallax—In tidal work, the term refers to horizontal parallax, which is the angle formed at the center of a celestial body between a line to the center of the Earth and a line tangent to the Earth's surface. Since the sine of a small angle is approximately equal to the angle itself in radians, it is usually taken in tidal work simply as the ratio of the mean radius of the Earth to the distance of the tide-producing body. Since the parallax is a function of the distance of a celestial body, the term is applied to tidal inequalities arising from the changing distance of the tide-producing body.

parallax inequality—The variation in the range of tide or in the speed of a tidal current due to changes in the distance of the Moon from the Earth. The range of tide and speed of the current tend alternately to increase and decrease as the Moon approaches its perigee and apogee, respectively, the complete cycle being the anomalistic month. There is a similar but relatively unimportant inequality due to the Sun, the cycle being the anomalistic year. The parallax has little direct effect upon the lunitidal intervals but tends to modify the phase effect. When the Moon is in perigee, the priming and lagging of the tide due to the phase is diminished and when in apogee the priming and lagging is increased.

parallax reduction—A processing of observed high and low waters to obtain quantities depending upon changes in the distance of the Moon, such as perigean and apogean ranges.

parallel plate intake—Intake of a stilling or protective well with two parallel plates attached below. The plates are typically three times the diameter of the well and are spaced three inches apart. The plates are used to minimize current-induced draw-down (Bernoulli effect) error in water level measurements.

pelorus—An instrument formerly used on a vessel in connection with a current line and current pole to obtain the set of the current. In its simplest form, it was a disk about 8 inches in diameter and graduated clockwise for every 5° or 10°. It was mounted rigidly on the vessel, usually with the 0° mark forward and the diameter through this mark parallel with the keel. Bearings were then related to the vessel's compass and converted to true.

perigean tides or tidal currents—Tides of increased range or tidal currents of increased speed occurring monthly as the result of the Moon being in perigee. The perigean range (Pn) of tide is the average range occurring at the time of perigean tides and is most conveniently computed from the harmonic constants. It is larger than the mean range where the type of tide is either semidiurnal or mixed, and is of no practical significance where the type of tide is predominantly diurnal.

perigee—The point in the orbit of the Moon or a man-made satellite nearest to the Earth. The point in the orbit of a satellite nearest to its companion body.

perihelion—The point in the orbit of the Earth (or other planet, etc.) nearest to the Sun.

period—Interval required for the completion of a recurring event, such as the revolution of a celestial body or the time between two consecutive like phases of the tide or tidal current. A period may be expressed in angular measure as 360°. The word also is used to express any specified duration of time.

permanent current—A current that runs continuously and is independent of tides and other temporary causes. Permanent currents include the general surface circulation of the oceans.

Peru Current—A South Pacific Ocean current setting northward along the west coast of South America. It has sometimes been called the Humboldt Current because an early record of its temperature was taken by the German scientist Alexander von Humboldt in 1802. It has also been called the Peruvian or Chilean Current. The name Corriente de Peru was adopted by a resolution of the Ibero-American Oceanographic Conference at its Madrid-Malaga meeting in April 1935.

phase—(1) Any recurring aspect of a periodic phenomenon, such as new Moon, high water, flood strength, etc. (2) A particular instant of a periodic function expressed in angular measure and reckoned from the time of its maximum value, the entire period of the function being 360°. The maximum and minimum of a harmonic constituent have phase values of 0° and 180°, respectively.

phase inequality—Variations in the tides or tidal currents due to changes in the phase of the Moon. At the times of new and full Moon the tide-producing forces of the Moon and Sun act in conjunction, causing the range of tide and speed of the tidal current to be greater than the average, the tides at these times being known as spring tides. At the times of the quadratures of the Moon these forces are opposed to each other, causing neap tides with diminished range and current speed.

phase lag—Same as epoch (1).

phase reduction—A processing of observed high and low waters to obtain quantities depending upon the phase of the Moon, such as the spring and neap ranges of tide. At a former time this process was known as second reduction. Also applicable to tidal currents.

pororoca—Brazilian for tidal bore.

PORTS—Physical Oceanographic Real Time System. A national system of current, water level, and other oceanographical and meteorological sensors telemetering data in real-time to central locations for storage, processing, and dissemination. Available to pilots, mariners, the U.S. Coast Guard, and other marine interests in voice or digital form. First introduced in Tampa Bay.

potential, tide-producing—Tendency for particles on the Earth to change their positions as a result of the gravitational interactions between the Sun, Moon, and Earth. Although gravitational attraction varies inversely as the square of the distance of the tide producing body, the resulting potential varies inversely as the cube of the distance.

predicting machine—See tide predicting machine.

pressure gauge—A water level gauge that is operated by the change in pressure at the bottom of a body of water due to the rise and fall of the water level. See gas purged pressure gauge.

pressure gradient force, horizontal—The horizontal component of the product of the specific volume and the rate of decrease in pressure with distance.

pressure sensor—A pressure transducer sensing device for water level measurement. A relative transducer is vented to the atmosphere and pressure readings are made relative to atmospheric pressure. An absolute transducer measures the pressure at its location. The readings are then corrected for barometric pressure taken at the surface.

primary control tide station—A tide station at which continuous observations have been made over a minimum of 19 years. Its purpose is to provide data for computing accepted values of the harmonic and nonharmonic constants essential to tide predictions and to the determination of tidal datums for charting and for coastal and marine boundaries. The data series from this station serves as a primary control for the reduction of relatively short series from subordinate tide stations through the method of comparison of simultaneous observations and for monitoring long-period sea level trends and variations. See tide station, secondary control tide station, tertiary tide station, and subordinate tide station (1).

primary tidal bench mark—See bench mark.

prime meridian—The meridian of longitude which passes through the original site of the Royal Observatory in Greenwich, England and used as the origin of longitude. Also known as the Greenwich Meridian.

priming of tide—The periodic acceleration in the time of occurrence of high and low waters due to changes in the relative positions of the Sun and Moon.

progressive wave—A wave that advances in distance along the sea surface or at some intermediate depth. Although the wave form itself travels significant distances, the water particles that make up the wave merely describe circular (in relatively deep water) or elliptical (in relatively shallow water) orbits. With high, steep, wind waves, a small overlap in the orbital motion becomes significant. This overlapping gives rise to a small net mass transport. See long shore current and rip current. Progressive waves can be internal, traveling along a sharp density discontinuity, such as the thermocline, or in a layer of gradually changing density (vertically).

protective well—A vertical pipe with a relatively large opening (intake) in the bottom. It is used with the air acoustic ranging sensor and electronic processing (filtering) technique to minimize the nonlinear characteristics of the stilling well. Its purpose is also to shield the sensing element from physical damage and harsh environment. Unlike a stilling well, damping of high frequency waves is not a critical requirement. See stilling well.

pycnocline—A layer in which the density increases significantly (relative to the layers above and below) with depth.

Q

Q_1—Larger lunar elliptic diurnal constituent. See M_1.
Speed = $T - 3s + h + p$ = 13.398,660,9° per solar hour.

$2Q_1$—Lunar elliptic diurnal, second order, constituent.
Speed = $T - 4s + h + 2p$ = 12.854,286,2° per solar hour.

quadrature of Moon—Position of the Moon when its longitude differs by 90° from the longitude of the Sun. The corresponding phases are known as first quarter and last quarter.

R

R_2—Smaller solar elliptic constituent. This constituent, with T_2, modulates the amplitude and frequency of S_2 for the effect of variation in the Earth's orbital speed due to its elliptical orbit.
Speed = $2T + h - p_1$ = 30.041,066,7° per solar hour.

race—A very rapid current through a comparatively narrow channel.

radiational tide—Periodic variations in sea level primarily related to meteorological changes such as the semidaily (solar) cycle in barometric pressure, daily (solar) land and sea breezes, and seasonal (annual) changes in temperature. Other changes in sea level due to meteorological changes that are random in phase are not considered radiational tides.

range of tide—The difference in height between consecutive high and low waters. The mean range is the difference in height between mean high water and mean low water. The great diurnal range or diurnal range is the difference in height between mean higher high water and mean lower low water. For other ranges see spring, neap, perigean, apogean, and tropic tides; and tropic ranges.

real-time—Pertains to a data collecting system that monitors an on-going process and disseminates measured values before they are expected to have changed significantly.

rectilinear current—Same as reversing current.

red tide (water)—The term applied to toxic algal blooms caused by several genera of dinoflagellates (*Gymnodinium* and *Gonyaulax*) which turn the sea red and are frequently associated with a deterioration in water quality. The color occurs as a result of the reaction of a red pigment, peridinin, to light during photosynthesis. These toxic algal blooms pose a serious threat to marine life and are potentially harmful to humans. The term has no connection with astronomic tides. However, its association with the word "tide" is from popular observations of its movements with tidal currents in estuarine waters.

reduction factor (F)—Reciprocal of node factor (f).

reduction of tides or tidal currents—A processing of observed tide or tidal current data to obtain mean values for tidal or tidal current constants.

reference station—A tide or current station for which independent daily predictions are given in the "Tide Tables" and "Tidal Current Tables," and from which corresponding predictions are obtained for subordinate stations by means of differences and ratios. See subordinate tide station (2) and subordinate current station (2).

relative mean sea level change—A local change in mean sea level relative to a network of bench marks established in the most stable and permanent material available (bedrock, if possible) on the land adjacent to the tide station location. A change in relative mean sea level may be composed of both an absolute mean sea level change component and a vertical land movement change component.

residual current—The observed current minus the astronomical tidal current.

response analysis—For any linear system, an input function $X_i(t)$ and an output function $X_0(t)$ can be related according to the formula:
$$X_0(t) = {_0}\int^\infty X_i(t - \tau)W(\tau)d\tau + noise(t)$$
where $W(\tau)$ is the impulse response of the system and its Fourier transform:
$$Z(f) = {_0}\int^\infty W(\tau)e^{-2\pi i f\tau} = R(f)e^{i\phi(f)}$$
is the system's admittance (coherent output/input) at

frequency f. In practice, the integrals are replaced by summations; X_i, W, and Z are generally complex. The discrete set of W values are termed response weights; $X_0(t)$ is ordinarily an observed tidal time series and $X_i(t)$ the tide potential or the tide at some nearby place. A future prediction can be prepared by applying the weights to an appropriate $X_i(t)$ series. In general:

$|Z| = R(f)$ and $Tan(Z) = \phi(f)$

measure the relative magnification and phase lead of the station at frequency f.

reversing current—A tidal current which flows alternately in approximately opposite directions with a slack water at each reversal of direction. Currents of this type usually occur in rivers and straits where the direction of flow is more or less restricted to certain channels. When the movement is towards the shore or up a stream, the current is said to be flooding, and when in the opposite direction, it is said to be ebbing. The combined flood and ebb movement (including the slack water) covers, on an average, 12.42 hours for a semidiurnal current. If unaffected by a nontidal flow, the flood and ebb movements will each last about 6 hours, but when combined with such a flow, the durations of flood and ebb may be quite different. During the flow in each direction the speed of the current will vary from zero at the time of slack water to a maximum about midway between the slacks.

reversing falls—A name applied to falls which flow alternately in opposite directions in a narrow channel in the St. John River above the city of St. John, New Brunswick, Canada, the phenomenon being due to the large range of tide and a constriction in the river. The direction of flow is upstream or downstream according to whether it is high or low water on the outside, the falls disappearing at the half-tide level.

rho (ρ_1)—Larger lunar evectional diurnal constituent. Speed = $T - 3s + 3h - p = 13.471,514,5°$ per solar hour.

rip—Agitation of water caused by the meeting of currents or by a rapid current setting over an irregular bottom. Termed tide rip when a tidal current is involved. See overfalls.

rip current—A narrow intense current setting seaward through the surf zone. It removes the excess water brought to the zone by the small net mass transport of waves. It is fed by longshore currents. Rip currents usually occur at points, groins, jetties, etc., of irregular beaches, and at regular intervals along straight, uninterrupted beaches.

river current—The gravity-induced seaward flow of fresh water originating from the drainage basin of a river. In the fresh water portion of the river below head of tide, the river current is alternately increased and decreased by the effect of the tidal current. After entering a tidal estuary, river current is the depth-averaged mean flow through any cross-section. See head of tide and estuary.

river estuary—See estuary.

rotary current—A tidal current that flows continually with the direction of flow changing through all points of the compass during the tidal period. Rotary currents are usually found offshore where the direction of flow is not restricted by any barriers. The tendency for the rotation in direction has its origin in the Coriolis force and, unless modified by local conditions, the change is clockwise in the Northern Hemisphere and counterclockwise in the Southern. The speed of the current usually varies throughout the tidal cycle, passing through the two maxima in approximately opposite directions and the two minima with the direction of the current at approximately 90° from the directions of the maxima.

S

s—Rate of change (as of January 1, 1900) in mean longitude of Moon. $s = 0.549,016,53°$ per solar hour.

S_1—Solar diurnal constituent. Speed = $T = 15.000,000,0°$ per solar hour.

S_2—Principal solar semidiurnal constituent. This constituent represents the rotation of the Earth with respect to the Sun. Speed = $2T = 30.000,000,0°$ per solar hour.

S_4, S_6—Shallow water overtides of the principal solar constituent. Speed of $S_4 = 2S_2 = 4T = 60.000,000,0°$ per solar hour. Speed of $S_6 = 3S_2 = 6T = 90.000,000,0°$ per solar hour.

Sa—Solar annual constituent. This constituent, with Ssa, accounts for the nonuniform changes in the Sun's declination and distance. In actuality, they mostly reflect yearly meteorological variations influencing sea level. Speed = $h = 0.041,068,64°$ per solar hour.

Ssa—Solar semiannual constituent. See Sa. Speed = $2h = 0.082,137,3°$ per solar hour.

salinity (S)—The total amount of solid material in grams contained in 1 kilogram of sea water when all the carbonate has been converted to oxide, the bromine and iodine replaced by chlorine, and all organic matter completely oxidized. The following is approximate. $S(‰) = 1.806,55 \times Cl(‰)$ Where $Cl(‰)$ is chlorinity in parts per thousand. See chlorinity.

Sargasso Sea—The west central region of the subtropical gyre of the North Atlantic Ocean. It is bounded by the North Atlantic, Canary, North Equatorial, and Antilles Currents, and the Gulf Stream. It is characterized by the absence of any well-marked currents and by large quantities of drifting Sargassum, or gulfweed.

Saros—A period of 223 synodic months corresponding approximately to 19 eclipse years or 18.03 Julian years, and is a cycle in which solar and lunar eclipses repeat themselves under approximately the same conditions.

sea level datum (SLD)—An obsolete term. See National Geodetic Vertical Datum of 1929 and mean sea level.

second reduction—Same as phase reduction.

secondary control tide station—A tide station at which continuous observations have been made over a minimum period of 1 year but less than 19 years. The series is reduced by comparison with simultaneous observations from a primary control tide station. This station provides for a 365-day harmonic analysis including the seasonal fluctuation of sea level. See tide station, primary control tide station, tertiary tide station, and subordinate tide station (1).

secular trend—See apparent secular trend as preferred term.

seiche—A stationary wave usually caused by strong winds and/or changes in barometric pressure. It is found in lakes, semi-enclosed bodies of water, and in areas of the open ocean. The period of a seiche in an enclosed rectangular body of water is usually represented by the formula:

Period $(T) = 2L / \sqrt{gd}$

in which L is the length, d the average depth of the body of water, and g the acceleration of gravity. See standing wave.

seismic sea wave—Same as tsunami.

semidiurnal—Having a period or cycle of approximately one-half of a tidal day. The predominant type of tide throughout the world is semidiurnal, with two high waters and two low waters each tidal day. The tidal current is said to be semidiurnal when there are two flood and two ebb periods each day. A semidiurnal constituent has two maxima and two minima each constituent day, and its symbol is the subscript 2. See type of tide.

sequence of current—The order of occurrence of the four tidal current strengths of a day, with special reference as to whether the greater flood immediately precedes or follows the greater ebb.

sequence of tide—The order in which the four tides of a day occur, with special reference as to whether the higher high water immediately precedes or follows the lower low water.

set (of current)—The direction towards which the current flows.

shallow water constituent—A short-period harmonic term introduced into the formula of tidal (or tidal current) constituents to account for the change in the form of a tide wave resulting from shallow water conditions. Shallow water constituents include the overtides and compound tides.

shallow water wave—A wave is classified as a shallow water wave whenever the ratio of the depth (the vertical distance of the still water level from the bottom) to the wave length (the horizontal distance between crests) is less than 0.04. Such waves propagate according to the formula:

$C = \sqrt{gd}$

where C is the wave speed, g the acceleration of gravity, and d the depth. Tidal waves are shallow water waves.

shear—A quasi-horizontal layer moving at a different velocity relative to the layer directly below and/or above.

shoreline (coastline)—The intersection of the land with the water surface. The shoreline shown on charts represents the line of contact between the land and a selected water elevation. In areas affected by tidal fluctuations, this line of contact is the mean high water line. In confined coastal waters of diminished tidal influence, the mean water level line may be used. See coast line.

sidereal day—The time of the rotation of the Earth with respect to the vernal equinox. It equals approximately 0.997,27 of a mean solar day. Because of the precession of the equinoxes, the sidereal day thus defined is slightly less than the period of rotation with respect to the fixed stars, but the difference is less than a hundredth part of a second.

sidereal month—Average period of the revolution of the Moon around the Earth with respect to a fixed star, equal to 27.321,661 mean solar days.

sidereal time—This is usually defined by astronomers as the hour angle of the vernal equinox. The sidereal day is the interval between two successive upper transits of the vernal equinox. It is to be noted that when applied to the month and year the word sidereal has reference to motion with respect to the fixed stars, while the word tropical is used for motion with respect to the vernal equinox. Because of the precession of the equinox there is a slight difference.

sidereal year—Average period of the revolution of the Earth around the Sun with respect to a fixed star. Its length is approximately 365.256,4 mean solar days.

sigma-t (σ_t)—An expression of density as a function of temperature and salinity (at atmospheric pressure) in a convenient numerical form. See density.

$\sigma_t = (\rho_{s,t,p} - 1)1,000$

sigma-zero (σ_o)—An expression of density as a function of salinity (at atmospheric pressure and 0°C) in a convenient numerical form. See density.

$\sigma_o = (\rho_{s,t,o} - 1)1,000$

slack; ebb begins (slack before ebb)—The slack water immediately preceding the ebb current.

slack; flood begins (slack before flood)—The slack water immediately preceding the flood current.

slack water (slack)—The state of a tidal current when its speed is near zero, especially the moment when a reversing current changes direction and its speed is zero. The term also is applied to the entire period of low speed near the time of turning of the current when it is too weak to be of any practical importance in navigation. The relation of the time of slack water to the tidal phases varies in different localities. For a perfect standing tidal wave, slack water occurs at the time of high and of low water, while for a perfect progressive tidal wave, slack water occurs midway between high and low water. See slack; ebb begins and slack; flood begins.

small diurnal range (Sl)—Difference in height between mean lower high water and mean higher low water.

small tropic range (Sc)—Difference in height between tropic lower high water and tropic higher low water.

solar day—The period of the rotation of the Earth with respect to the Sun. The mean solar day is the time of the rotation with respect to the mean Sun. The solar day commencing at midnight is called a civil or calendar day, but if the day is reckoned from noon it is known as an astronomical day because of its former use in astronomical calculation.

solar tide—(1) The part of the tide that is due to the tide-producing force of the Sun. (2) The observed tide in areas where the solar tide is dominant. This condition provides for phase repetition at about the same time each solar day.

solar time—Time measured by the hour angle of the Sun. It is called apparent time when referred to the actual Sun and mean time when referred to the mean Sun. It is also classified as local, standard, or Greenwich according to whether it is reckoned from the local, standard, or Greenwich meridian.

solitary wave—A wave of translation consisting of a single crest rising above the undisturbed water level without any accompanying trough. The rate of advance of a solitary wave depends upon the depth of the water and is usually expressed by the formula:

$$C = \sqrt{g(d + h)}$$

in which C = rate of advance, g = acceleration of gravity, d = depth of water, and h = height of wave, the depth and height being measured from the undisturbed water level.

solstices—The two points in the ecliptic where the Sun reaches its maximum and minimum declinations; also the times when the Sun reaches these points. The maximum north declination occurs on or near June 21, marking the beginning of summer in the Northern Hemisphere and the beginning of winter in the Southern. The maximum south declination occurs on or near December 22, marking the beginning of winter in the Northern Hemisphere and the beginning of summer in the Southern.

solstitial tides—Tides occurring near the times of the solstices. The tropic range may be expected to be especially large at these times.

Somali (East Africa Coast) Current—An Indian Ocean current setting southwestward along the coast of Somalia. The current reverses and sets to the northeast during the Southwest Monsoon.

South Equatorial Current—A current setting westward along and south of the Equator in the Atlantic and Pacific Oceans, and south of the Equator in the Indian Ocean. It occurs immediately south of the Equatorial Counter Current.

Southwest Monsoon Current—Same as Monsoon Current.

species of constituent—A classification depending upon the period of a constituent. The principal species are semidiurnal, diurnal, and long-period.

specific volume anomaly, or steric anomaly (δ)—The excess in specific volume over the standard specific volume at 35 ‰, 0°C, and the given pressure. See thermosteric anomaly and specific volume.

$$\delta = \alpha_{s,t,p} - \alpha_{35,o,p}$$

specific volume, in situ ($\alpha_{s,t,p}$)—Volume per unit mass. The reciprocal of density (specific gravity). The specific volume of sea water as a function of salinity, temperature, and pressure. See specific volume anomaly and thermosteric anomaly.

speed (of constituent)—The rate of change in the phase of a constituent, usually expressed in degrees per hour. The speed is equal to 360° divided by the constituent period expressed in hours.

speed (of current)—The magnitude of velocity. Rate at which the current flows. Usually expressed in knots or centimeters per second.

Spitsbergen Atlantic Current—A current setting northwestward off the southwest coast of Spitsbergen in the Greenland Sea.

spring high water—Same as mean high water springs (MHWS). See spring tides.

spring low water—Same as mean low water springs (MLWS). See spring tides and mean low water springs.

spring range (Sg)—See spring tides.

spring tides or tidal currents—Tides of increased range or tidal currents of increased speed occurring semimonthly as the result of the Moon being new or full. The spring range (Sg) of tide is the average range occurring at the time of spring tides and is most conveniently computed from the harmonic constants. It is larger than the mean range where the type of tide is either semi diurnal or mixed, and is of no practical significance where the type of tide is predominantly diurnal. The average height of the high waters of the spring tides is called spring high water or mean high water springs (MHWS) and the average height of the corresponding low waters is called spring low water or mean low water springs (MLWS).

stand of tide—Sometimes called a platform tide. An interval at high or low water when there is no sensible change in the height of the tide. The water level is stationary at high and low water for only an instant, but the change in level near these times is so slow that it is not usually perceptible. In general, the duration of the apparent stand will depend upon the range of tide, being longer for a small range than for a large range, but where there is a tendency for a double tide the stand may last for several hours even with a large range of tide.

standard method—A tidal datum computation method. Generally used for the West Coast and Pacific Island stations. Values needed are mean tide level (MTL), mean range of tide (MN), great diurnal range (GT), and mean diurnal high and low water inequalities (DHQ and DLQ) as determined by comparison with an appropriate control. From those, the following are computed:

MLW = MTL - (0.5*MN)
MHW = MLW + MN
MLLW = MLW - DLQ
MHHW = MHW + DHQ

standard time—A kind of time based upon the transit of the Sun over a certain specified meridian, called the time meridian, and adopted for use over a considerable area. With a few exceptions, standard time is based upon some meridian which differs by a multiple of 15° from the meridian of Greenwich. The United States first adopted standard time in 1883 on the initiative of the American Railway Association, and at noon on November 18 of that year the telegraphic time signals from the Naval Observatory at Washington were changed to this system.

standing (stationary) wave—A wave that oscillates without progressing. One-half of such a wave may be illustrated by the oscillation of the water in a pan that has been tilted. Near the axis, which is called the node or nodal line, there is no vertical rise and fall of the water. The ends of the wave are called loops and at these places the vertical rise and fall is at a maximum. The current is maximum near the node and minimum at the loops. The period of a stationary wave depends upon the length and depth of the body of water and, for a simple rectangular basin, may be expressed by the formula:

$$T = 2L / \sqrt{gd}$$

in which T is the period of wave, L the length of the basin, d the depth of water, and g the acceleration of gravity. A stationary wave may be resolved into two progressive waves of equal amplitude and equal speeds moving in opposite directions.

station datum—See datum of tabulation.

stationary wave theory—An assumption that the basic tidal movement in the open ocean consists of a system of stationary wave oscillations, any progressive wave movement being of secondary importance except as the tide advances into tributary waters. The continental masses divide the sea into irregular basins, which, although not completely enclosed, are capable of sustaining oscillations which are more or less independent. The tide-producing force consists principally of two parts, a semidiurnal force with a period of approximately half a day and a diurnal force with a period of approximately a whole day. Insofar as the free period of oscillation of any part of the ocean, as determined by its dimensions and depth, is in accord with the semidiurnal or diurnal tide-producing forces, there will be built up corresponding oscillations of considerable amplitude which will be manifested in the rise and fall of the tide. The diurnal oscillations, superimposed upon the semidiurnal oscillations, cause the inequalities in the heights of the two high and the two low waters of each day. Although the tidal movement as a whole is somewhat complicated by the overlapping of oscillating areas, the theory is consistent with observational data.

stencils—Perforated sheets formerly used with the tabulated hourly heights of the tide or speeds of the tidal current for the purpose of distributing and grouping them into constituent hours preliminary to summing for harmonic analysis. See Coast and Geodetic Survey Special Publication No. 98, Manual of Harmonic Analysis and Prediction of Tides. This analysis is now performed on electronic digital computers.

steric anomaly—Same as specific volume anomaly.

stilling well—A vertical pipe with a relatively small opening (intake) in the bottom. It is used in a gauge installation to dampen short period surface waves while freely admitting the tide, other long period waves, and sea level variations; which can then be measured by a water level gauge sensor inside. See float well and protective well.

storm surge—The local change in the elevation of the ocean along a shore due to a storm. The storm surge is measured by subtracting the astronomic tidal elevation from the total elevation. It typically has a duration of a few hours. Since wind generated waves ride on top of the storm surge (and are not included in the definition), the total instantaneous elevation may greatly exceed the predicted storm surge plus astronomic tide. It is potentially catastrophic, especially on low lying coasts with gently sloping offshore topography. See storm tide.

storm tide—As used by the National Weather Service, NOAA, the sum of the storm surge and astronomic tide. See storm surge.

stray line—Ungraduated portion of line connected with the current pole formerly used in taking current observations. The stray line was usually about 100 feet long and permitted the pole to acquire the velocity of the current at some distance from the disturbed waters in the immediate vicinity of the observing vessel, before the current velocity was read from the graduated portion of the current line.

strength of current—Phase of tidal current in which the speed is a maximum; also the speed at this time. Beginning with slack before flood in the period of a reversing tidal current (or minimum before flood in a rotary current), the speed gradually increases to flood strength and then diminishes to slack before ebb (or minimum before ebb in a rotary current), after which the current turns in direction, the speed increases to ebb strength and then diminishes to slack before flood, completing the cycle. If it is assumed that the speed throughout the cycle varies as the ordinates of a cosine curve, it can be shown that the average speed for an entire flood or ebb period is equal to $2/\pi$ or 0.636,6 of the speed of the corresponding strength of current.

strength of ebb—Same as ebb strength.

strength of flood—Same as flood strength.

submerged lands—Lands covered by water at any stage of the tide. See tidelands.

subordinate current station—(1) A current station from which a relatively short series of observations is reduced by comparison with simultaneous observations from a control current station. See current station, control current station, and reference station. (2) A station listed in the Tidal Current Tables for which predictions are to be obtained by means of differences and ratios applied to the full predictions at a reference station. See reference station.

subordinate tide station—(1) A tide station from which a relatively short series of observations is reduced by comparison with simultaneous observations from a tide station with a relatively long series of observations. See tide station, primary control tide station, secondary control tide station, and tertiary tide station. (2) A station listed in the Tide Tables from which predictions are to be obtained by means of differences and ratios applied to the full predictions at a reference station. See reference station.

summer time—British name for daylight saving time.

synodical month—The average period of the revolution of the Moon around the Earth with respect to the Sun, or the average interval between corresponding phases of the Moon. The synodical month is approximately 29.530,588 days in length.

syzygy—With respect to tides, whenever the Moon is lined up with the Earth and Sun in a straight Sun-Moon-Earth or Sun-Earth-Moon configuration. At these times the range of tide is greater than average. See spring tides or tidal currents.

T

T—Rate of change of hour angle of mean Sun at place of observation.
$T = 15°$ per mean solar hour.

T_2—Larger solar elliptic constituent. See R_2.
Speed = $2T - h + p_1 = 29.958,933,3°$ per solar hour.

tape gauge—See electric tape gauge.

telemetry—The capability of transmitting or retrieving data over long distance communication links, such as satellite, VHF radio, or telephone.

terdiurnal—Having three periods in a constituent day. The symbol of a terdiurnal constituent is the subscript 3.

tertiary tide station—A tide station at which continuous observations have been made over a minimum period of 30 days but less than 1 year. The series is reduced by comparison with simultaneous observations from a secondary control tide station. This station provides for a 29-day harmonic analysis. See tide station, primary control tide station, secondary control tide station, and subordinate tide station (1).

thermocline—A layer in which the temperature decreases significantly (relative to the layers above and below) with depth. The principal ones are designated diurnal, seasonal, and main thermocline.

thermosteric anomaly$(\delta_T, \Delta', \text{ or } \Delta_{s,t})$—The specific volume anomaly (steric anomaly) that would be attained if the water were changed isothermally to a standard pressure of one atmosphere. The specific volume anomaly with pressure terms omitted. See isanostere.

tidal bench mark—See bench mark.

tidal bench mark description—A published, concise description of the location, stamped number or designation, date established, and elevation (referred to a tidal datum) of a specific bench mark.

tidal bench mark state index map—A state map which indicates the locations for which tidal datums and tidal bench mark descriptions are available.

tidal bore—A tidal wave that propagates up a relatively shallow and sloping estuary or river with a steep wave front. The leading edge presents an abrupt rise in level, frequently with continuous breaking and often immediately followed by several large undulations. An uncommon phenomenon, the tidal bore is usually associated with very large ranges in tide as well as wedge shaped and rapidly shoaling entrances. Also called eagre, eager (for Tsientan, China bore), mascaret (French), pororoca (Brazilian), and bore.

tidal characteristics—Principally, those features relating to the time, range, and type of tide.

tidal constants—Tidal relations that remain practically constant for any particular locality. Tidal constants are classified as harmonic and nonharmonic. The harmonic constants consist of the amplitudes and epochs of the harmonic constituents, and the nonharmonic constants include the ranges and intervals derived directly from the high and low water observations.

tidal constituent—See constituent.

tidal current—A horizontal movement of the water caused by gravitational interactions between the Sun, Moon, and Earth. The horizontal component of the particulate motion of a tidal wave. Part of the same general movement of the sea that is manifested in the vertical rise and fall called tide. The United States equivalent of the British tidal stream. See tidal wave, tide, and current.

Tidal Current Chart Diagrams—A series of monthly diagrams to be used with the Tidal Current Charts. Each diagram contains lines that indicate the specific tidal current chart to use for a given date and time, and the speed factor to apply to that chart.

Tidal Current Charts—Charts on which tidal current data are depicted. Tidal Current Charts for a number of important waterways are published by the National Ocean Service. Each consists of a set of charts giving the speed and direction of the current for each hour or equal interval of the tidal cycle, thus presenting a comprehensive view of the tidal current movement.

tidal current constants—See current constants.

tidal current station—See current station.

Tidal Current Tables—Tables which give daily predictions of the times and velocities of the tidal currents. These predictions are usually supplemented by current differences and constants through which predictions can be obtained for numerous other locations.

tidal datum—See datum.

tidal day—Same as lunar day.

tidal difference—Difference in time or height between a high or low water at a subordinate station and a reference station for which predictions are given in the Tide Tables. The difference, when applied according to sign to the prediction at the reference station, gives the corresponding time or height for the subordinate station.

tidal epoch—See National Tidal Datum Epoch and epoch.

tidal estuary—See estuary.

tidal stream—British equivalent of United States tidal current.

tidal wave—A shallow water wave caused by the gravitational interactions between the Sun, Moon, and Earth. Essentially, high water is the crest of a tidal wave and low water, the trough. Tidal current is the horizontal component of the particulate motion, while tide is manifested by the vertical component. The observed tide and tidal current can be considered the result of the combination of several tidal waves, each of which may vary from nearly pure progressive to nearly pure standing and with differing periods, heights, phase relationships, and direction.

tidal zoning—The practice of dividing a hydrographic survey area into discrete zones or sections, each one possessing similar tidal characteristics. One set of tide reducers is assigned to each zone. Tide reducers are used to adjust the soundings in that zone to chart datum (MLLW). Tidal zoning is necessary in order to correct for differing water level heights occurring throughout the survey area at any given time. Each zone of the survey area is geographically delineated such that the differences in time and range do not exceed certain limits, generally 0.2 hours and 0.2 feet respectively; however, these limits are subject to change depending upon type of survey, location, and tidal characteristics. The tide reducers are derived from the water levels recorded at an appropriate tide station, usually nearby. Tide reducers are used to correct the soundings throughout the hydrographic survey area to a common, uniform, uninterrupted chart datum. See tide reducers.

tide—The periodic rise and fall of a body of water resulting from gravitational interactions between Sun, Moon, and Earth. The vertical component of the particulate motion of a tidal wave. Although the accompanying horizontal movement of the water is part of the same phenomenon, it is preferable to designate this motion as tidal current. See tidal wave.

tide curve—A graphic representation of the rise and fall of the tide in which time is usually represented by the abscissa and height by the ordinate. For a semidiurnal tide with little diurnal inequality, the graphic representation approximates a cosine curve. See marigram.

tide datum—See datum.

tide (water level) gauge—An instrument for measuring the rise and fall of the tide (water level). See ADR gauge, automatic tide gauge, Next Generation Water Level Measurement System, gas purged pressure gauge, electric tape gauge, pressure gauge, and tide staff.

tide predicting machine—A mechanical analog machine especially designed to handle the great quantity of constituent summations required in the harmonic method. William Ferrel's Maxima and Minima Tide Predictor (described in Manual of Tides, U.S. Coast and Geodetic Survey, Appendix 10, Report for 1883) was the first such machine used in the United States. Summing only 19 constituents, but giving direct readings of the predicted times and heights of the high and low waters, the Ferrel machine was used for the predictions of 1885 through 1914. A second machine, developed by Rollin A. Harris and E. G. Fischer and summing 37 constituents, was used for the predictions of 1912 through 1965 (described in Manual of Harmonic Analysis and Prediction of Tides by Paul Schureman, U.S. Coast and Geodetic Survey Special Publication No. 98, 1958). Predictions are now prepared using an electronic digital computer.

tide-producing force—That part of the gravitational attraction of the Moon and Sun which is effective in producing the tides on the Earth. The force varies approximately as the mass of the attracting body and inversely as the cube of its distance. The tide-producing force exerted by the Sun is a little less than one-half as great as that of the Moon. A mathematical development of the vertical and horizontal components of the tide-producing forces of the Moon and Sun will be found in Coast and Geodetic Survey Special Publication No. 98.

tide reducers—Height corrections for reducing soundings to chart datum (MLLW). A tide reducer represents the height of the water level at a given place and time relative to chart datum. Tide reducers are obtained from one or more tide stations within or nearby the survey area. Often, due to differing tidal characteristics over the survey area, the tide reducers obtained directly from a tide station must be corrected to adjust for time and range of tide differences in the various zones of the hydrographic survey area. See tidal zoning.

tide rip—See rip.

tide staff—A water level gauge consisting of a vertical graduated staff from which the height of the water level can be read directly. It is called a fixed staff when secured in place so that it cannot be easily removed. A portable staff is one that is designed for removal from the water when not in use. For such a staff a fixed support is provided. The support has a metal stop secured to it so that the staff will always have the same elevation when installed for use. See electric tape gauge.

tide (water level) station—The geographic location at which tidal observations are conducted. Also, the facilities used to make tidal observations. These may include a tide house, tide (water level) gauge, tide staff, and tidal bench marks. See primary control tide station, secondary control tide station, tertiary tide station, and subordinate tide station (1).

Tide Tables—Tables which give daily predictions of the times and heights of high and low waters. These predictions are usually supplemented by tidal differences and constants through which predictions can be obtained for numerous other locations.

tide wave—See tidal wave.

tidelands—The zone between the mean high water and mean low water lines. It is identical with intertidal zone (technical definition) when the type of tide is semidiurnal or diurnal.

tidewater—Water activated by the tide generating forces and/or water affected by the resulting tide, especially in coastal and estuarine areas. Also, a general term often applied to the land and water of estuarine areas formed by postglacial drowning of coastal plain rivers.

tideway—A channel through which a tidal current flows.

time—Time is measured by the rotation of the Earth with respect to some point in the celestial sphere and may be designated as sidereal, solar, or lunar, according to whether the measurement is taken in reference to the vernal equinox, the Sun, or the Moon. Solar time may be apparent or mean, according to whether the reference is to the actual Sun or the mean Sun. Mean solar time may be local or standard, according to whether it is based upon the transit of the Sun over the local meridian or a selected meridian adopted as a standard over a considerable area. Greenwich time is standard time based upon the meridian of Greenwich. In civil time the day commences at midnight, while in astronomical time, as used prior to 1925, the beginning of the day was reckoned from noon of the civil day of the same date. The name universal time is now applied to Greenwich mean civil time.

time meridian—A meridian used as a reference for time.

total current—The combination of the tidal and non-tidal current. The United States equivalent of the British flow. See current.

tractive force—The horizontal component of a tide-producing force vector (directed parallel with level surfaces at that geographic location).

transit—The passage of a celestial body over a specified meridian. The passage is designated as upper transit or lower transit according to whether it is over that part of the meridian lying above or below the polar axis.

tropic currents—Tidal currents occurring semi-monthly when the effect of the Moon's maximum declination is greatest. At these times the tendency of the Moon to produce a diurnal inequality in the current is at a maximum.

tropic inequalities—Tropic high water inequality (HWQ) is the average difference between the two high waters of the day at the times of tropic tides. Tropic low water inequality (LWQ) is the average difference between the two low waters of the day at the times of tropic tides.

These terms are applicable only when the type of tide is semidiurnal or mixed. See tropic tides.

tropic intervals—Tropic higher high water interval (TcHHWI) is the lunitidal interval pertaining to the higher high waters at the time of the tropic tides. Tropic lower low water interval (TcLLWI) is the lunitidal interval pertaining to the lower low waters at the time of the tropic tides. Tropic intervals are marked a when reference is made to the upper transit of the Moon at its north declination or to the lower transit at the time of south declination, and are marked b when the reference is to the lower transit at the north declination or to the upper transit at the south declination. See tropic tides.

tropic ranges—The great tropic range (Gc), or tropic range, is the difference in height between tropic higher high water and tropic lower low water. The small tropic range (Sc) is the difference in height between tropic lower high water and tropic higher low water. The mean tropic range (Mc) is the mean between the great tropic and the small tropic range. Tropic ranges are most conveniently computed from the harmonic constants. See tropic tides.

tropic speed—The greater flood or greater ebb speed at the time of tropic currents.

tropic tides—Tides occurring semimonthly when the effect of the Moon's maximum declination is greatest. At these times there is a tendency for an increase in the diurnal range. The tidal datums pertaining to the tropic tides are designated as tropic higher high water (TcHHW), tropic lower high water (TcLHW), tropic higher low water (TcHLW), and tropic lower low water (TcLLW).

tropical month—The average period of the revolution of the Moon around the Earth with respect to the vernal equinox. Its length is approximately 27.321,582 days.

tropical year—The average period of the revolution of the Earth around the Sun with respect to the vernal equinox. Its length is approximately 365.242,2 days. The tropical year determines the cycle of changes in the seasons, and is the unit to which the calendar year is adjusted through the occasional introduction of the extra day on leap years.

trough—The lowest point in a propagating wave. See low water and tidal wave.

true direction—Direction relative to true north (0°) which is the direction of the north geographic pole. See compass direction and magnetic direction.

tsunami—A shallow water progressive wave, potentially catastrophic, caused by an underwater earthquake or volcano.

Tsushima Current—A North Pacific Ocean current setting northeastward in the East China Sea (in summer) and Sea of Japan. A segment of the Kuroshio System.

type of tide—A classification based on characteristic forms of a tide curve. Qualitatively, when the two high waters and two low waters of each tidal day are approximately equal in height, the tide is said to be semidiurnal; when there is a relatively large diurnal inequality in the high or low waters or both, it is said to be mixed; and when there is only one high water and one low water in each tidal day, it is said to be diurnal. Quantitatively (after Dietrich), where the amplitude ratio of $K_1 + O_1$ to $M_2 + S_2$ is less than 0.25, the tide is classified as semidiurnal; where the ratio is from 0.25 to 1.5, the tide is mixed, mainly semidiurnal; where the ratio is from 1.5 to 3.0, the tide is mixed, mainly diurnal; and where greater than 3.0, diurnal.

U

universal time (UT)—Same as Greenwich mean time (GMT). See time, kinds.

uplands— Land above the mean high water line (shoreline) and subject to private ownership, as distinguished from tidelands, the ownership of which is prima facie in the state but also subject to divestment under state statutes. See tidelands.

upwelling—An upward flow of subsurface water due to such causes as surface divergence, offshore wind, and wind drift transport away from shore.

V

$V_0 + u$—See equilibrium argument.

vanishing tide—In a predominantly mixed tide with a very large diurnal inequality, the lower high water and higher low water become indistinct (or vanish) at times of extreme declinations.

variation (of compass)—Difference between true north as determined by the Earth's axis of rotation and magnetic north as determined by the Earth's magnetism. Variation is designated as east or positive when the magnetic needle is deflected to the east of true north and as west or negative when the deflection is to the west of true north. The variation changes with time. Also called magnetic declination.

variational inequality—An inequality in the Moon's motion due mainly to the tangential component of the Sun's attraction.

velocity (of current)—Speed and set of the current.

vernal equinox—See equinoxes.

vulgar establishment—Same as establishment of the port.

W

water level gauge—See tide gauge.

water level station—See tide station.

wave height—The vertical distance between crest and trough. See range of tide.

West Australian Current—An Indian Ocean current setting northward along the west coast of Australia.

West Greenland Current—A North Atlantic Ocean current setting northward along the west coast of Greenland.

West Wind Drift—Same as Antarctic Circumpolar Current.

wind drift—An ocean current in which only the Coriolis and frictional forces are significant. The wind drift embodies an Ekman spiral.

Z

Z_0—Symbol recommended by the International Hydrographic Organization to represent the elevation of mean sea level above chart datum.